ONE POT MEALS

SHEET PAN, SKILLET & DUTCH OVEN RECIPES

pil

Publications International, Ltd.

ISBN: 978-1-68022-077-3

Library of Congress Control Number: 2015938822

Manufactured in China.

8 7 6 5 4 3 2 1

Preparation/Cooking Times: Preparation times are based on the approximate amount of time required to assemble the recipe before cooking, baking, chilling or serving. These times include preparation steps such as measuring, chopping and mixing. The fact that some preparations and cooking can be done simultaneously is taken into account. Preparation of optional ingredients and serving suggestions is not included.

Publications International, Ltd.

Table of Contents

Cast Iron Entrées

Lemon Garlic Roast Chicken

4 sprigs fresh rosemary, divided

6 cloves garlic, divided

1 lemon

2 tablespoons butter, softened

2 teaspoons salt, divided

2 large russet potatoes, peeled and cut into ¾-inch pieces

2 onions, cut into 1-inch pieces

2 tablespoons olive oil

½ teaspoon black pepper

1 whole chicken (3 to 4 pounds)

1. Preheat oven to 400°F. Finely chop 2 sprigs of rosemary (about 2 tablespoons). Mince 3 cloves garlic. Grate peel from lemon. Combine butter, chopped rosemary, minced garlic, lemon peel and ½ teaspoon salt in small bowl; mix well. Set aside while preparing vegetables.

2. Combine potatoes, onions, oil, 1 teaspoon salt and pepper in medium bowl; toss to coat. Spread mixture in single layer in large cast iron skillet.

3. Smash remaining 3 cloves garlic. Cut lemon into quarters. Season cavity of chicken with remaining ½ teaspoon salt. Place garlic, lemon quarters and remaining 2 sprigs of rosemary in cavity; tie legs with kitchen string, if desired. Place chicken on top of vegetables in skillet; spread butter mixture over chicken.

4. Roast about 1 hour or until chicken is cooked through (165°F) and potatoes are tender. Let stand 10 minutes before carving. Sprinkle with additional salt and pepper to taste.

Makes 4 servings

Ham and Barbecued Bean Skillet

1 tablespoon vegetable oil

1 cup chopped onion

1 teaspoon minced garlic

1 can (about 15 ounces) kidney beans, rinsed and drained

1 can (about 15 ounces) cannellini or Great Northern beans, rinsed and drained

1 cup chopped green bell pepper

½ cup packed brown sugar

½ cup ketchup

2 tablespoons cider vinegar

2 teaspoons dry mustard

1 ham steak (½ inch thick, about 12 ounces)

1. Heat oil in large cast iron skillet over medium-high heat. Add onion and garlic; cook and stir 4 minutes or until onion is translucent. Add kidney beans, cannellini beans, bell pepper, brown sugar, ketchup, vinegar and mustard; mix well.

2. Trim fat from ham; cut ham into ½-inch pieces. Add ham to skillet. Reduce heat to low; simmer about 10 minutes or until sauce thickens and mixture is heated through, stirring occasionally.

Makes 4 servings

Southern Fried Catfish with Hush Puppies

2 cups yellow cornmeal, divided

½ cup plus 3 tablespoons all-purpose flour, divided

2 teaspoons baking powder

2 teaspoons salt, divided

1 cup milk

1 small onion, minced

1 egg, lightly beaten

4 catfish fillets (about 1½ pounds)

¼ teaspoon ground red pepper

Vegetable oil for frying

1. Combine 1½ cups cornmeal, ½ cup flour, baking powder and ½ teaspoon salt in medium bowl. Stir in milk, onion and egg until well blended. Let batter stand 5 to 10 minutes before frying.

2. Rinse catfish; pat dry with paper towels. Combine remaining ½ cup cornmeal, 3 tablespoons flour, 1½ teaspoons salt and red pepper in shallow dish. Dip fish into cornmeal mixture, shaking off excess. Heat 1 inch oil in large cast iron skillet over medium heat until 375°F on deep-fry thermometer.

3. Cook fish in batches 4 to 5 minutes or until golden brown and fish begins to flake when tested with fork. Drain fish on paper towel-lined plate; keep warm. *Allow temperature of oil to return to 375°F between batches.*

4. For hush puppies, drop batter by tablespoonfuls into hot oil (375°F). Fry in batches 2 minutes or until golden brown. Drain on paper towel-lined plate.

Makes 4 servings

BBQ Chicken Skillet Pizza

1 pound frozen bread
  dough, thawed

1 tablespoon olive oil

2 cups shredded cooked
  chicken*

¾ cup barbecue sauce,
  divided

¼ cup (1 ounce) shredded
  mozzarella cheese

¼ cup thinly sliced red onion

½ cup (2 ounces) shredded
  smoked Gouda cheese

Chopped fresh cilantro
  (optional)

*Use a rotisserie chicken for best flavor
and convenience.

1. Preheat oven to 425°F. Roll out dough into 15-inch circle on lightly floured surface. Brush oil over bottom and side of large (12-inch) cast iron skillet; place in oven 5 minutes to preheat.

2. Combine chicken and ½ cup barbecue sauce in medium bowl; toss to coat. Carefully remove hot skillet from oven; press dough into bottom and about 1 inch up side of skillet.

3. Spread remaining ¼ cup barbecue sauce over dough. Sprinkle with mozzarella; top with chicken mixture. Sprinkle with half of onion and Gouda; top with remaining onion.

4. Bake about 25 minutes or until crust is golden brown. Garnish with cilantro.

Makes 4 to 6 servings

Skillet Mac and Cheese

1 pound uncooked cavatappi or rotini pasta

8 ounces thick-cut bacon, cut into ½-inch pieces

¼ cup finely chopped onion

¼ cup all-purpose flour

3½ cups whole milk

1 cup (4 ounces) shredded white Cheddar cheese

1 cup (4 ounces) shredded fontina cheese

1 cup (4 ounces) shredded Gruyère cheese

¾ cup grated Parmesan cheese, divided

½ teaspoon salt

½ teaspoon dry mustard

¼ teaspoon ground red pepper

¼ teaspoon black pepper

¼ cup panko bread crumbs

1. Preheat oven to 400°F. Cook pasta in large saucepan according to package directions until al dente; drain.

2. Meanwhile, cook bacon in large cast iron skillet until crisp; drain on paper towel-lined plate. Pour drippings into glass measuring cup, leaving thin coating on surface of skillet.

3. Heat 4 tablespoons drippings in large saucepan over medium-high heat. Add onion; cook and stir about 4 minutes or until translucent. Add flour; cook and stir 5 minutes. Reduce heat to medium-low; gradually add milk, stirring constantly. Stir in Cheddar, fontina, Gruyère, ½ cup Parmesan, salt, mustard, red pepper and black pepper until smooth and well blended. Add cooked pasta; stir gently until coated. Stir in bacon. Spread mixture in cast iron skillet.

4. Combine panko and remaining ¼ cup Parmesan in small bowl; sprinkle over pasta. Bake about 30 minutes or until top is golden brown.

Makes 6 servings

Spanish-Style Paella

- 6 cups chicken stock or broth
- 3 tablespoons olive oil
- ½ pound boneless skinless chicken thighs, cut into bite-size pieces
- 2 to 3 links chorizo sausage (about 5 ounces), sliced
- 1 medium onion, chopped
- 1 red bell pepper, chopped
- 4 cloves garlic, minced
- 1 teaspoon saffron threads, minced
- 1½ cups uncooked rice
- 1 can (10 ounces) diced tomatoes with chiles
- 3 tablespoons tomato paste
- ½ teaspoon salt
- ¼ teaspoon black pepper
- 1 pound large raw shrimp, peeled and deveined (with tails on)
- ½ pound mussels
- ½ cup frozen peas, thawed

1. Bring stock to a boil in medium saucepan over high heat; keep warm over low heat.

2. Heat oil in large cast iron skillet over medium-high heat. Add chicken and chorizo; cook 1 minute, stirring once. Add onion, bell pepper, garlic and saffron; cook and stir 5 minutes or until vegetables are soft and chorizo is browned.

3. Stir in rice, diced tomatoes, tomato paste, salt and black pepper until blended; cook 5 minutes, stirring occasionally. Add stock, ½ to 1 cup at a time, stirring after each addition until stock is almost absorbed.

4. Reduce heat to medium. Cover skillet with foil; cook 25 to 30 minutes or until rice is tender. Remove foil; gently stir in shrimp, mussels and peas. Replace foil; cook 5 to 10 minutes or until shrimp are pink and opaque and mussels open.

Makes 6 to 8 servings

Ham and Cheddar Frittata

3 eggs

3 egg whites

½ teaspoon salt

½ teaspoon black pepper

1½ cups (4 ounces) frozen
broccoli florets, thawed

6 ounces smoked ham,
cut into ½-inch cubes
(1¼ cups)

⅓ cup roasted red peppers,
cut into thin strips

1 tablespoon butter

½ cup (2 ounces) shredded
sharp Cheddar cheese

1. Preheat broiler.

2. Beat eggs, egg whites, salt and black pepper in large bowl until well blended. Stir in broccoli, ham and roasted pepper.

3. Melt butter in large (10-inch) cast iron skillet over medium heat. Pour egg mixture into skillet; cover and cook 5 to 6 minutes or until eggs are set around edge. (Center will be wet.)

4. Sprinkle cheese over frittata. Transfer skillet to broiler; broil, uncovered, 5 inches from heat, 2 minutes or until eggs are set in center and cheese is melted. Let stand 5 minutes before serving.

Makes 4 servings

Mexican Tamale Skillet Casserole

- 1 pound ground chuck
- 1 cup frozen corn, thawed
- 1 can (8 ounces) tomato sauce
- ½ cup water
- 1 can (4 ounces) diced green chiles
- 1 package (1¼ ounces) taco seasoning mix
- ½ teaspoon ground cumin
- 1 cup milk
- 2 eggs
- ½ cup biscuit baking mix
- 1½ cups (6 ounces) shredded Monterey Jack cheese or Mexican cheese blend
- Sour cream, sliced black olives, chopped tomatoes and chopped fresh cilantro (optional)

1. Preheat oven to 400°F. Brown beef in large cast iron skillet over medium-high heat 6 to 8 minutes, stirring to break up meat. Drain fat; return beef to skillet.

2. Stir in corn, tomato sauce, water, chiles, taco seasoning and cumin; mix well. Remove from heat; smooth top of mixture into even layer with spoon.

3. Combine milk, eggs and baking mix in medium bowl; stir until well blended. Pour over beef mixture in skillet.

4. Bake 40 minutes or until crust is golden and knife inserted into center comes out clean. Sprinkle with cheese; let stand 5 minutes before serving. Garnish as desired.

Makes 4 servings

Chicken Scarpiello

3 tablespoons extra virgin olive oil, divided

1 pound spicy Italian sausage, cut into 1-inch pieces

1 (3-pound) whole chicken, cut into 10 pieces*

1 teaspoon salt, divided

1 large onion, chopped

2 red or orange bell peppers, cut into 1/4-inch strips

3 cloves garlic, minced

1/2 cup dry white wine such as sauvignon blanc

1/2 cup chicken broth

1/2 cup coarsely chopped seeded hot cherry peppers

1/2 cup liquid from cherry pepper jar

1 teaspoon dried oregano

Additional salt and black pepper

1/4 cup chopped fresh Italian parsley

*Or purchase 2 bone-in chicken breasts and 2 chicken leg quarters; cut breasts in half and separate drumsticks and thighs.

1. Heat 1 tablespoon oil in large cast iron skillet over medium-high heat. Add sausage; cook about 10 minutes or until well browned on all sides, stirring occasionally. Remove to plate.

2. Heat 1 tablespoon oil in same skillet. Sprinkle chicken with 1/2 teaspoon salt; arrange skin side down in single layer in skillet (cook in batches if necessary). Cook about 6 minutes per side or until browned. Remove to plate. Drain fat from skillet.

3. Heat remaining 1 tablespoon oil in skillet. Add onion and remaining 1/2 teaspoon salt; cook and stir 2 minutes or until onion is softened, scraping up browned bits from bottom of skillet. Add bell peppers and garlic; cook and stir 5 minutes. Stir in wine; cook until liquid is reduced by half. Stir in broth, cherry peppers, cherry pepper liquid, oregano and additional salt and black pepper to taste; bring to a simmer.

4. Return sausage and chicken to skillet along with any accumulated juices. Partially cover and simmer 10 minutes. Remove cover; simmer 15 minutes or until chicken is cooked through (165°F). Sprinkle with parsley.

Makes 4 to 6 servings

Pan-Roasted Pike with Buttery Bread Crumbs

6 tablespoons butter, divided

2 cloves garlic, minced

⅓ cup plain dry bread crumbs

½ teaspoon salt, divided

4 tablespoons chopped fresh parsley

4 pike fillets or other medium-firm white fish (about 6 ounces each)

⅛ teaspoon black pepper

2 tablespoons lemon juice

1. Preheat oven to 400°F.

2. Melt 2 tablespoons butter in small nonstick skillet over medium-high heat. Add garlic; cook and stir 1 minute or just until lightly browned. Add bread crumbs and ⅛ teaspoon salt; cook and stir 1 minute. Transfer to small bowl; stir in parsley.

3. Melt 1 tablespoon butter in large cast iron skillet over medium-high heat. Sprinkle pike with ¼ teaspoon salt and pepper. Add to skillet, flesh side down; cook 1 minute. Remove from heat; turn fish and top with bread crumb mixture. Transfer to oven; roast 8 to 10 minutes or until fish begins to flake when tested with fork.

4. Wipe out small skillet with paper towel; heat over medium heat. Add remaining 3 tablespoons butter; cook 3 to 4 minutes or until melted and lightly browned, stirring occasionally. Stir in lemon juice and remaining ⅛ teaspoon salt. Spoon mixture over fish just before serving.

Makes 4 servings

Pizza Casserole

2 cups uncooked rotini or other spiral pasta

1½ pounds ground beef

1 medium onion, chopped

Salt and black pepper

1 can (about 15 ounces) pizza sauce

1 can (8 ounces) tomato sauce

1 can (6 ounces) tomato paste

½ teaspoon sugar

½ teaspoon garlic salt

½ teaspoon dried oregano

2 cups (8 ounces) shredded mozzarella cheese

12 to 15 slices pepperoni

1. Preheat oven to 350°F. Cook pasta according to package directions until al dente; drain.

2. Meanwhile, brown beef with onion in large skillet over medium-high heat 6 to 8 minutes, stirring to break up meat. Drain fat. Season with salt and pepper.

3. Combine pasta, pizza sauce, tomato sauce, tomato paste, sugar, garlic salt and oregano in large bowl; mix well. Add beef mixture; stir until blended.

4. Spread half of mixture in large cast iron skillet; sprinkle with 1 cup cheese. Repeat layers. Top with pepperoni.

5. Bake 25 to 30 minutes or until heated through and cheese is melted.

Makes 6 servings

Pork Chop and Stuffing Skillet

4 thin bone-in pork chops (4 ounces each)	2 cups corn bread stuffing mix
¼ teaspoon dried thyme	1 cup diced green bell pepper
¼ teaspoon paprika	⅛ to ¼ teaspoon poultry seasoning (optional)
⅛ teaspoon salt	1¼ cups water
1 tablespoon olive oil	
4 ounces bulk pork sausage	

1. Preheat oven to 350°F. Sprinkle one side of pork chops with thyme, paprika and salt. Heat oil in large cast iron skillet over medium-high heat. Add pork, seasoned side down; cook 2 minutes. Remove to plate; keep warm.

2. Add sausage to skillet; cook until no longer pink, stirring to break up meat. Remove from heat; stir in stuffing mix, bell pepper, poultry seasoning, if desired, and water just until blended. Arrange pork, seasoned side up, over stuffing mixture.

3. Cover and bake 15 minutes or until pork is barely pink in center. Let stand 5 minutes before serving.

Makes 4 servings

Tortilla Chicken Skillet

Prep Time: 15 minutes   **Start to Finish Time:** 30 minutes

- 1 tablespoon vegetable oil
- 1 pound boneless skinless chicken breasts, diced
- 1 cup diced onions
- 2 cups ORTEGA® Salsa Verde
- 1 cup frozen corn
- 4 (8-inch) ORTEGA® Flour Soft Tortillas, cut into strips
- 1 can (4 ounces) ORTEGA® Diced Jalapeños
- 1 cup prepared queso sauce or cheese sauce
- ¼ cup chopped fresh cilantro (optional)

PREHEAT oven to 350°F.

HEAT oil in large ovenproof skillet over medium-high heat until hot. Add chicken and onions; cook and stir 5 minutes or just until chicken begins to brown.

ADD salsa verde, corn, tortilla strips and jalapeños; stir until well combined. Stir in queso sauce.

BAKE 15 minutes or until bubbly and heated through. Garnish with cilantro, if desired.

Makes 6 servings

Tip: If you don't have an ovenproof skillet, pour the chicken mixture into a casserole dish before baking.

Baked Pasta and Cheese Supreme

8 ounces uncooked fusilli or other spiral pasta

12 slices bacon, diced

½ medium onion, chopped

2 cloves garlic, minced

2 teaspoons dried oregano, divided

1 can (8 ounces) tomato sauce

1 teaspoon hot pepper sauce (optional)

1½ cups (6 ounces) shredded Cheddar or Colby cheese

½ cup fresh bread crumbs (from 1 slice of white bread)

1 tablespoon butter, melted

1. Preheat oven to 400°F. Cook pasta according to package directions until al dente; drain and keep warm.

2. Meanwhile, cook bacon in large cast iron skillet over medium heat until crisp. Drain on paper towel-lined plate.

3. Add onion to bacon drippings in skillet; cook and stir 3 minutes or until onion is translucent. Stir in garlic and 1 teaspoon oregano; cook and stir 1 minute. Stir in tomato sauce and hot pepper sauce, if desired. Add cooked pasta and cheese; stir gently until coated.

4. Combine bacon, bread crumbs, butter and remaining 1 teaspoon oregano in small bowl; sprinkle over pasta mixture. Bake 10 minutes or until hot and bubbly.

Makes 4 servings

Spinach and Turkey Skillet

8 ounces turkey breast
   tenderloin or turkey
   strips

¼ teaspoon salt

1 tablespoon olive oil

¼ cup chopped onion

2 cloves garlic, minced

⅓ cup uncooked rice

¾ teaspoon Italian
   seasoning

¼ teaspoon black pepper

1 cup reduced-sodium
   chicken broth, divided

2 cups packed fresh spinach

⅔ cup diced plum tomatoes

3 tablespoons grated
   Parmesan cheese

1. Cut turkey into bite-size pieces; sprinkle with salt.

2. Heat oil in medium cast iron skillet over medium-high heat. Add turkey; cook and stir until lightly browned. Remove to plate. Add onion and garlic to skillet; cook and stir over medium heat until tender. Return turkey to skillet; stir in rice, Italian seasoning and pepper.

3. Reserve 2 tablespoons broth. Stir remaining broth into mixture in skillet; bring to a boil. Reduce heat to low; cover and simmer 14 minutes.

4. Stir in spinach and reserved broth; cover and cook 2 to 3 minutes or until liquid is absorbed and spinach is wilted. Stir in tomatoes; heat through. Sprinkle with cheese.

Makes 2 servings

Baked Chicken and Garlic Orzo

1 tablespoon plus
  1 teaspoon olive oil,
  divided

4 bone-in chicken breasts,
  skin removed

1 cup chopped onion

¼ cup dry white wine

10 ounces uncooked orzo
  pasta

1 can (about 14 ounces)
  chicken broth

¼ cup water

2 tablespoons chopped
  fresh parsley

4 cloves garlic, minced

1 teaspoon dried oregano

1 teaspoon lemon-pepper
  seasoning, divided

¾ teaspoon salt

  Paprika

1 lemon, cut into wedges

1. Preheat oven to 350°F. Heat 1 tablespoon oil in large cast iron skillet over high heat. Add chicken, meat side down; cook 1 to 2 minutes without moving or until lightly browned. Remove to plate.

2. Add onion to skillet; cook and stir over medium-high heat 2 minutes or until softened. Add wine; cook 30 seconds or until slightly reduced, scraping up browned bits from bottom of skillet.

3. Stir in orzo, broth, water, parsley, garlic, oregano, ½ teaspoon lemon-pepper seasoning and salt; mix well. Arrange chicken breasts over orzo; sprinkle with remaining ½ teaspoon lemon-pepper seasoning and paprika.

4. Bake, uncovered, 1 hour or until cooked through (165°F). Remove chicken from skillet; stir remaining 1 teaspoon oil into orzo mixture. Serve with lemon wedges.

Makes 4 servings

Hearty Sausage & Rice Skillet

Prep Time: 15 minutes   Bake Time: 15 minutes

1 pound bulk pork sausage

1 package (8 ounces) sliced mushrooms

2 stalks celery, coarsely chopped

1 large red pepper, coarsely chopped

1 large onion, coarsely chopped (about 1 cup)

1 teaspoon dried thyme leaves, crushed

½ teaspoon dried marjoram leaves, crushed

1 box (6 ounces) long-grain white and wild rice blend

1¾ cups SWANSON® Chicken Broth (Regular, Natural Goodness® or Certified Organic)

1 can (10¾ ounces) CAMPBELL'S® Condensed Cream of Mushroom Soup (Regular **or** 98% Fat Free)

1 cup shredded Cheddar cheese (4 ounces)

1. Cook the sausage in a 12-inch oven-safe skillet over medium-high heat until the sausage is well browned, stirring frequently to separate the meat. Pour off any fat.

2. Add the mushrooms, celery, pepper, onion, thyme, marjoram and seasoning packet from the rice blend and cook until the vegetables are tender-crisp. Stir in the broth, soup, rice blend and ½ **cup** of the cheese. **Cover.**

3. Bake at 375°F. for 1 hour or until hot and bubbly and the rice is tender. Uncover and stir. Sprinkle with the remaining cheese.

Makes 6 servings

Kitchen Tip: To protect skillet handle, cover with foil.

Skillet Suppers

Easy Skillet Chicken Pot Pie

1 can (10¾ ounces) reduced-sodium cream of chicken soup, undiluted	2 cups diced cooked chicken
	½ teaspoon black pepper
1¼ cups milk, divided	1 cup biscuit baking mix
1 package (10 ounces) frozen mixed vegetables	¼ teaspoon dried summer savory leaves or parsley (optional)

1. Combine soup, 1 cup milk, vegetables, chicken and pepper in medium skillet; bring to a boil over medium heat.

2. Meanwhile, combine baking mix and summer savory, if desired, in small bowl. Stir in remaining 3 to 4 tablespoons milk just until soft batter forms.

3. Drop 6 tablespoonfuls batter over chicken mixture; cover loosely and simmer 12 minutes or until dumplings are cooked through, spooning liquid over dumplings once or twice during cooking.

Makes 6 servings

Soba Stir-Fry

8 ounces uncooked soba (buckwheat) noodles

1 tablespoon olive oil

2 cups sliced shiitake mushrooms

1 medium red bell pepper, cut into thin strips

2 whole dried red chiles *or* ¼ teaspoon red pepper flakes

1 clove garlic, minced

2 cups shredded napa cabbage

½ cup reduced-sodium vegetable broth

2 tablespoons reduced-sodium tamari or soy sauce

1 tablespoon rice wine or dry sherry

2 teaspoons cornstarch

1 package (14 ounces) firm tofu, drained and cut into 1-inch cubes

2 green onions, thinly sliced

1. Cook noodles according to package directions; drain and set aside.

2. Heat oil in large nonstick skillet over medium-high heat. Add mushrooms, bell pepper, dried chiles and garlic; cook and stir 3 minutes or until mushrooms are tender. Add cabbage; cover and cook 2 minutes or until cabbage is wilted.

3. Whisk broth, tamari and rice wine into cornstarch in small bowl until smooth. Stir sauce into vegetable mixture; cook 2 minutes or until sauce is thickened.

4. Stir in tofu and noodles; toss gently until heated through. Sprinkle with green onions. Serve immediately.

Makes 4 servings

Bratwurst Skillet

1 pound bratwurst links, cut into ½-inch slices

1½ cups *each* red and green bell pepper strips

1½ cups sliced onions

1 teaspoon paprika

1 teaspoon caraway seeds

1. Heat large skillet over medium heat. Add bratwurst; cover and cook about 5 minutes or until browned and no longer pink in center. Remove to plate; keep warm.

2. Drain all but 1 tablespoon drippings from skillet. Add bell peppers, onions, paprika and caraway seeds; cook and stir about 5 minutes or until vegetables are tender. Return bratwurst to skillet; cook and stir just until heated through.

Makes 4 servings

Quick Skillet Supper

½ pound beef sirloin steak

1 tablespoon vegetable oil

2 cups (about 8 ounces) sliced fresh mushrooms

1 can (17 ounces) whole kernel corn, drained

1 can (14½ ounces) stewed tomatoes, undrained

1 clove garlic, minced

1 teaspoon dried oregano leaves

⅛ teaspoon ground black pepper

3 cups hot cooked rice

Partially freeze steak; slice across the grain into ⅛-inch strips. Heat oil in large skillet over medium-high heat until hot. Brown meat quickly in oil, about 2 minutes; remove from skillet. Add vegetables, garlic, oregano and pepper; cook and stir 1 minute. Reduce heat to medium; cover and cook 4 to 6 minutes. Return meat to skillet and cook until heated through. Serve over rice.

Makes 6 servings

*Favorite recipe from **USA Rice Federation**®*

Bratwurst Skillet

Pork Chops with Red Pepper and Sweet Potato

4 pork loin chops,
½ inch thick (about
4 ounces each)

1 teaspoon lemon-pepper
seasoning

1 tablespoon vegetable
or canola oil

½ cup water

1 tablespoon lemon juice

1 teaspoon dried fines
herbes, crushed

½ teaspoon beef bouillon
granules

1¼ cups red and/or yellow
bell pepper strips

1 cup sliced peeled sweet
potato, cut into 1-inch
pieces

¾ cup sliced onion

4 cups hot cooked rice

1. Trim fat from pork chops. Rub both sides of pork with lemon-pepper seasoning. Heat oil in large skillet over medium-high heat. Add pork; cook 5 minutes or until browned on both sides.

2. Combine water, lemon juice, fines herbes and bouillon granules in small bowl; mix well. Pour mixture over pork in skillet. Reduce heat to medium-low; cover and simmer 5 minutes.

3. Add bell peppers, sweet potato and onion to skillet; bring to a boil. Reduce heat to low; cover and simmer 10 to 15 minutes or until pork is barely pink in center and vegetables are crisp-tender. Remove pork and vegetables to plate; keep warm.

4. Bring remaining juices in skillet to a boil over high heat. Reduce heat to medium; cook and stir until mixture slightly thickens, stirring occasionally. Serve pork, vegetables and sauce over rice.

Makes 4 servings

Tuscan Turkey and White Bean Skillet

- 1 teaspoon dried rosemary, divided
- ½ teaspoon garlic salt
- ½ teaspoon black pepper, divided
- 1 pound turkey breast cutlets, pounded to ¼-inch thickness
- 2 teaspoons olive oil, divided
- 1 can (about 15 ounces) navy beans or Great Northern beans, rinsed and drained
- 1 can (about 14 ounces) fire-roasted diced tomatoes
- ¼ cup grated Parmesan cheese

1. Combine ½ teaspoon rosemary, garlic salt and ¼ teaspoon pepper in small bowl; mix well. Sprinkle over turkey.

2. Heat 1 teaspoon oil in large nonstick skillet over medium heat. Add half of turkey; cook 2 to 3 minutes per side or until no longer pink in center. Remove to plate; cover to keep warm. Repeat with remaining 1 teaspoon oil and turkey.

3. Add beans, tomatoes, remaining ½ teaspoon rosemary and ¼ teaspoon pepper to skillet; bring to a boil over high heat. Reduce heat to low; simmer 5 minutes.

4. Serve turkey with bean mixture; sprinkle with cheese.

Makes 6 servings

Fish Tacos with Cilantro Cream Sauce

½ cup sour cream

¼ cup chopped fresh cilantro

1¼ teaspoons ground cumin, divided

1 pound skinless tilapia, mahimahi or other firm white fish fillets

1 teaspoon chipotle hot pepper sauce, divided

1 teaspoon garlic salt

2 teaspoons canola or vegetable oil

1 red bell pepper, cut into strips

1 green bell pepper, cut into strips

8 corn tortillas, warmed

4 limes, cut into wedges

1. Combine sour cream, cilantro and ¼ teaspoon cumin in small bowl; mix well. Refrigerate until ready to serve.

2. Cut tilapia into 1-inch chunks; place in medium bowl. Add ½ teaspoon hot pepper sauce, remaining 1 teaspoon cumin and garlic salt; toss gently to coat.

3. Heat oil in large nonstick skillet over medium heat. Add fish; cook 3 to 4 minutes or until center is opaque, turning gently. Remove to plate. Add bell peppers to skillet; cook and stir 6 to 8 minutes or until tender. Return fish to skillet with remaining ½ teaspoon hot pepper sauce; cook and stir just until heated through.

4. Spoon mixture into warm tortillas. Serve with sauce and lime wedges.

Makes 4 servings

Chicken and Herb Stew

½ cup all-purpose flour

½ teaspoon salt

¼ teaspoon black pepper

¼ teaspoon paprika

4 chicken drumsticks

4 chicken thighs

2 tablespoons olive oil

12 ounces new potatoes, quartered

2 carrots, quartered lengthwise and cut into 3-inch pieces

1 green bell pepper, cut into thin strips

¾ cup chopped onion

2 cloves garlic, minced

1¾ cups water

¼ cup dry white wine

2 cubes chicken bouillon

1 tablespoon chopped fresh oregano

1 teaspoon chopped fresh rosemary leaves

2 tablespoons chopped fresh Italian parsley (optional)

1. Combine flour, salt, black pepper and paprika in shallow dish; mix well. Coat chicken with flour mixture, shaking off excess.

2. Heat oil in large skillet over medium-high heat. Add chicken; cook 8 minutes or until browned on both sides, turning once. Remove to plate.

3. Add potatoes, carrots, bell pepper, onion and garlic to skillet; cook and stir 5 minutes or until lightly browned. Add water, wine and bouillon; cook 1 minute, stirring to scrape up browned bits from bottom of skillet. Stir in oregano and rosemary.

4. Place chicken on top of vegetable mixture, turning several times to coat. Cover and simmer 45 to 50 minutes or until chicken is cooked through (165°F), turning occasionally. Garnish with parsley.

Makes 4 servings

Bacon and Potato Frittata

5 eggs

½ cup crumbled crisp-
   cooked bacon

¼ cup half-and-half or milk

⅛ teaspoon salt

⅛ teaspoon black pepper

3 tablespoons butter

2 cups frozen O'Brien hash
   brown potatoes with
   onions and peppers

1. Preheat broiler. Beat eggs in medium bowl. Add bacon, half-and-half, salt and pepper; beat until well blended.

2. Melt butter in large ovenproof skillet over medium-high heat. Add potatoes; cook and stir 4 minutes. Pour egg mixture into skillet. Reduce heat to medium; cover and cook 6 minutes or until eggs are set at edges (center will still be wet).

3. Transfer skillet to broiler. Broil 4 inches from heat source 1 to 2 minutes or until top is golden brown and until center is set.

Makes 4 to 6 servings

Skillet Lasagna with Vegetables

½ pound hot Italian turkey sausage, casings removed

½ pound ground turkey

2 stalks celery, sliced

⅓ cup chopped onion

2 cups marinara sauce

1⅓ cups water

4 ounces uncooked bowtie pasta

1 medium zucchini, halved lengthwise and cut into ½-inch-thick slices (2 cups)

¾ cup chopped green or yellow bell pepper

½ cup ricotta cheese

2 tablespoons finely grated Parmesan cheese

½ cup (2 ounces) shredded mozzarella cheese

1. Cook and stir sausage, turkey, celery and onion in large skillet over medium-high heat until turkey is no longer pink.

2. Stir in marinara sauce and water; bring to a boil. Stir in pasta; cover and cook over medium-low heat 12 minutes.

3. Stir in zucchini and bell pepper; cover and simmer 2 minutes. Remove cover; simmer 4 to 6 minutes or until vegetables are crisp-tender.

4. Meanwhile, combine ricotta and Parmesan in small bowl. Drop by rounded teaspoonfuls over mixture in skillet. Sprinkle with mozzarella. Remove from heat; cover and let stand 10 minutes.

Makes 6 servings

Pepper Steak

- 2 cups MINUTE® White Rice, uncooked
- 1 boneless beef sirloin steak (1 pound), ½ inch thick, fat trimmed*
- ½ teaspoon garlic powder
- ¼ teaspoon black pepper
- 1 tablespoon vegetable oil
- 1 medium green bell pepper, cut into strips
- 1 medium red bell pepper, cut into strips
- 1 medium onion, sliced (optional)
- 1 cup reduced-sodium teriyaki sauce
- 1 tablespoon cornstarch

*Or substitute 1 pound boneless skinless chicken breasts.

Prepare rice according to package directions.

Slice steak into thin strips; season with garlic powder and pepper.

Heat oil in large nonstick skillet over medium-high heat. Add beef; cook and stir 4 to 5 minutes or until cooked through. Add bell pepper and onion, if desired, and cook until crisp-tender.

Combine teriyaki sauce and cornstarch, and add to beef mixture. Bring to a boil, stirring constantly. Simmer 2 minutes or until sauce thickens slightly. Serve over rice.

Makes 4 servings

Pork and Sweet Potato Skillet

1 tablespoon plus
   1 teaspoon butter,
   divided

12 ounces pork tenderloin,
   cut into 1-inch pieces

¼ teaspoon salt

⅛ teaspoon black pepper

2 medium sweet potatoes,
   peeled and cut into
   ½-inch pieces (about
   2 cups)

1 onion, sliced

¼ pound smoked turkey
   sausage, halved
   lengthwise and cut
   into ½-inch pieces

1 small green or red apple,
   peeled and cut into
   ½-inch pieces

½ cup prepared sweet-and-
   sour sauce

2 tablespoons chopped
   fresh parsley (optional)

1. Melt 1 teaspoon butter in large nonstick skillet over medium-high heat. Add pork; cook and stir 2 to 3 minutes or until no longer pink. Season with salt and pepper. Remove to plate.

2. Add remaining 1 tablespoon butter, sweet potatoes and onion to skillet; cook and stir over medium-low heat 8 to 10 minutes or until sweet potatoes are tender.

3. Return pork to skillet with sausage, apple and sweet-and-sour sauce; cook and stir until heated through. Garnish with parsley.

Makes 4 servings

Tre Formaggi Frittata

Prep Time: 15 minutes   **Cook Time:** 20 minutes

10 eggs

¼ cup grated Parmesan cheese

¼ teaspoon black pepper

1 teaspoon olive oil

4 JOHNSONVILLE® Mild Italian Sausage Links

1 cup thinly sliced green onions

¼ cup diced red bell pepper

3 cloves garlic, minced

1 teaspoon chopped fresh thyme *or* ½ teaspoon dried thyme

2 ounces Asiago cheese, cut into ½-inch cubes

4 ounces provolone cheese, cut into ½-inch cubes

1. Preheat oven to 350°F. Whisk together eggs, Parmesan cheese and black pepper in large bowl; set aside.

2. Heat oil in large ovenproof skillet over medium-high heat. Add sausage; cook, turning frequently, 5 to 7 minutes or until browned on all sides and cooked through (160°F). Transfer sausage to cutting board; when cool enough to handle, cut into coins.

3. Drain all but 1 teaspoon drippings from skillet; return to medium heat. Add green onions and bell pepper; cook and stir 2 minutes or until tender. Add garlic and thyme; cook and stir 30 seconds. Stir in sausage slices. Add egg mixture; cook 30 seconds without stirring or until egg mixture begins to set.

4. Stir in Asiago cheese and provolone cheese. Cook 2 minutes, gently lifting edges of mixture to allow uncooked egg mixture to reach pan bottom. Cook 4 minutes without stirring.

5. Transfer skillet to oven; bake 6 to 10 minutes or until center is firm and edges are golden brown. Gently shake pan to loosen frittata; carefully slide onto serving plate. Cut into wedges to serve.

Makes 6 to 8 servings

Easy Halibut Steaks with Tomato and Broccoli Sauce

2 tablespoons olive oil

2 cups chopped fresh broccoli

2½ cups diced fresh tomatoes

2 tablespoons lemon juice

1 tablespoon chopped garlic

1 tablespoon chopped fresh tarragon *or* 1 teaspoon dried tarragon

½ teaspoon sugar

½ teaspoon salt

½ teaspoon black pepper

4 halibut steaks (4 ounces each)

Lemon wedges (optional)

1. Heat oil in large skillet over medium heat. Add broccoli; cook and stir 5 minutes. Add tomatoes, lemon juice, garlic, tarragon, sugar, salt and pepper; cook and stir 5 minutes.

2. Add halibut to skillet; cover and cook 10 minutes or until fish begins to flake when tested with fork.

3. Divide vegetables evenly among four plates; top with fish. Serve with lemon wedges, if desired.

Makes 4 servings

Italian Country-Style Braised Chicken

¾ cup boiling water

½ cup dried porcini mushrooms (about ½ ounce)

¼ cup all-purpose flour

1 teaspoon salt

½ teaspoon black pepper

1 whole cut-up chicken (3½ to 4 pounds)

3 tablespoons olive oil

2 ounces pancetta or bacon, chopped

1 medium onion, chopped

2 carrots, thinly sliced

3 cloves garlic, minced

1 cup chicken broth

1 tablespoon tomato paste

1 cup pitted green Italian olives

1. Combine boiling water and mushrooms in small bowl. Let stand 15 to 20 minutes or until mushrooms are tender.

2. Meanwhile, combine flour, salt and pepper in large resealable food storage bag. Add two pieces of chicken at a time; toss to coat. Discard any remaining flour mixture.

3. Heat oil in large skillet over medium heat. Add chicken; cook until browned on both sides. Remove to plate.

4. Drain all but 1 tablespoon fat from skillet. Add pancetta, onion and carrots; cook 5 minutes, stirring occasionally to scrape up browned bits from bottom of skillet. Add garlic; cook and stir 1 minute.

5. Drain mushrooms, reserving liquid. Chop mushrooms; strain soaking liquid. Add mushrooms and liquid to skillet. Stir in broth and tomato paste; bring to a boil over high heat.

6. Return chicken to skillet along with any accumulated juices. Reduce heat to low; simmer 20 minutes or until chicken is cooked through (165°F) and sauce thickens, turning once. Add olives; cook and stir until heated through. Remove chicken to serving platter; top with sauce.

Makes 4 to 6 servings

Sweet Potato and Turkey Sausage Hash

1 link mild or hot turkey Italian sausage (about 4 ounces)

1 tablespoon olive oil

1 small red onion, finely chopped

1 small red bell pepper, finely chopped

1 small sweet potato, peeled and cut into ½-inch cubes

¼ teaspoon salt

¼ teaspoon black pepper

⅛ teaspoon ground cumin

⅛ teaspoon chipotle chili powder

1. Remove sausage from casing; shape sausage into ½-inch balls.

2. Heat oil in large skillet over medium heat. Add sausage; cook and stir 3 to 5 minutes or until browned. Remove to plate.

3. Add onion, bell pepper, sweet potato, salt, black pepper, cumin and chili powder to skillet; cook and stir 6 to 8 minutes or until sweet potato is tender.

4. Stir in sausage; cook without stirring 5 minutes or until hash is lightly browned.

Makes 2 servings

Tip: For a heartier main dish, serve the hash with a fried or poached egg on top.

Savory Pork Stir-Fry

Prep Time: 15 minutes

1 pound lean boneless
 pork loin

1 tablespoon vinegar

1 tablespoon soy sauce

1 teaspoon sesame oil

1 clove garlic, minced

½ teaspoon ground ginger

1 teaspoon vegetable oil

1 (10-ounce) package
 frozen stir-fry
 vegetables, unthawed

1 tablespoon chicken broth
 or water

Hot cooked rice (optional)

1 tablespoon toasted
 sesame seeds (optional)

Slice pork across grain into ⅛-inch strips. Marinate in vinegar, soy sauce, sesame oil, garlic and ginger for 10 minutes. Heat vegetable oil in nonstick pan until hot. Add pork mixture and stir-fry for 3 to 5 minutes, until pork is no longer pink. Add vegetables and chicken broth. Stir mixture, cover and steam until vegetables are crisp-tender. Serve over hot cooked rice and sprinkle with toasted sesame seeds, if desired.

Makes 4 servings

Favorite recipe from **National Pork Board**

Baking Dish Dinners

Baked Gnocchi

1 package (about 17 ounces) gnocchi

⅓ cup olive oil

3 cloves garlic, minced

1 package (10 ounces) frozen spinach, thawed and squeezed dry

1 can (about 14 ounces) diced tomatoes

1 teaspoon Italian seasoning

Salt and black pepper

½ cup grated Parmesan cheese

½ cup (2 ounces) shredded mozzarella cheese

1. Preheat oven to 350°F. Spray 2½-quart baking dish with nonstick cooking spray.

2. Cook gnocchi according to package directions; drain and set aside.

3. Meanwhile, heat oil in large skillet over medium heat. Add garlic; cook and stir 30 seconds. Stir in spinach; cover and cook 2 minutes or until spinach wilts. Add tomatoes, Italian seasoning, salt and pepper; cook and stir about 5 minutes. Gently stir in gnocchi. Spoon mixture into prepared baking dish; sprinkle with Parmesan and mozzarella.

4. Bake 20 to 30 minutes or until bubbly and cheese is melted.

Makes 4 to 6 servings

Huevos Rancheros Casserole

- 6 corn tortillas
- 1 cup refried black beans
- 1 cup salsa
- 10 eggs
- ¾ cup milk
- 1 cup (4 ounces) shredded Mexican cheese blend

1. Preheat oven to 400°F. Spray 13×9-inch baking dish with nonstick cooking spray.

2. Line prepared baking dish with tortillas, overlapping as necessary. Spread beans evenly over tortillas; top with salsa.

3. Whisk eggs and milk in large bowl until blended. Pour over tortillas and beans; sprinkle with cheese. Cover baking dish with foil.

4. Bake 30 minutes. Remove foil; bake 5 minutes or until center is set and edges are lightly browned and pulling away from sides of dish.

Makes 6 to 8 servings

Tip: When you have leftover refried beans, store them in a covered container in the refrigerator (not in the can). Use them in breakfast burritos, chicken or vegetable tostadas, quick-to-fix cheese quesadillas or spread over a crust in a Mexican pizza.

Cajun Chicken and Rice

4 chicken drumsticks, skin removed

4 chicken thighs, skin removed

2 teaspoons Cajun seasoning

¾ teaspoon salt

2 tablespoons vegetable oil

1 can (about 14 ounces) chicken broth

1 cup uncooked rice

1 medium green bell pepper, coarsely chopped

1 medium red bell pepper, coarsely chopped

½ cup finely chopped green onions

2 cloves garlic, minced

½ teaspoon dried thyme

¼ teaspoon ground turmeric

1. Preheat oven to 350°F. Spray 2- to 3-quart or 13×9-inch baking dish with nonstick cooking spray.

2. Pat chicken dry. Sprinkle both sides with Cajun seasoning and salt. Heat oil in large skillet over medium-high heat. Add chicken; cook 8 to 10 minutes or until browned all both sides. Remove to plate.

3. Add broth to skillet; bring to a boil, scraping up browned bits from bottom of skillet. Add rice, bell peppers, green onions, garlic, thyme and turmeric; mix well. Pour into prepared baking dish; arrange chicken on top. Cover with foil.

4. Bake 1 hour or until chicken is cooked through (165°F).

Makes 6 servings

Easy Pumpkin-Pasta Bake

Prep Time: 15 minutes   **Cook Time:** 25 minutes

Nonstick cooking spray

1 box (14½ ounces) whole wheat penne or other short-cut pasta, prepared according to package directions

1 pound (about 4 links) sweet or spicy lean Italian turkey sausage, casings removed

1 tablespoon finely chopped garlic

1 jar (24 to 26 ounces) marinara sauce

½ cup water or dry red or white wine

1 can (15 ounces) LIBBY'S® 100% Pure Pumpkin

4 tablespoons (¾ ounce) shredded Parmesan cheese, *divided*

1 cup (4 ounces) shredded low-moisture part-skim mozzarella cheese

PREHEAT oven to 375°F. Spray 3-quart casserole dish or 13×9-inch baking dish with nonstick cooking spray.

COOK sausage in large skillet over medium-high heat until cooked through. Stir in garlic; cook for 1 minute. Stir in marinara sauce (reserve jar). Add water or wine to jar; cover and shake. Pour into skillet along with pumpkin and *2 tablespoons* Parmesan cheese. Stir well. Stir in prepared pasta. Spoon into prepared dish. Sprinkle with *remaining 2 tablespoons* Parmesan cheese and mozzarella cheese; cover.

BAKE for 15 minutes. Carefully remove cover; bake for an additional 5 minutes or until cheese is melted and bubbly.

Makes 10 servings

Reuben Noodle Bake

8 ounces uncooked
egg noodles

5 ounces thinly sliced
deli-style corned beef

2 cups (8 ounces) shredded
Swiss cheese

1 can (about 14 ounces)
sauerkraut with caraway
seeds, drained

½ cup Thousand Island
dressing

½ cup milk

1 tablespoon prepared
mustard

2 slices pumpernickel bread

1 tablespoon butter, melted

1. Preheat oven to 350°F. Spray 13×9-inch baking dish with nonstick cooking spray. Cook noodles according to package directions; drain.

2. Meanwhile, cut corned beef into bite-size pieces. Combine noodles, corned beef, cheese and sauerkraut in large bowl; mix gently. Spoon into prepared baking dish.

3. Combine dressing, milk and mustard in small bowl; mix well. Spoon evenly over noodle mixture.

4. Tear bread into large pieces; process in food processor or blender until crumbs form. Add butter; pulse to combine. Sprinkle over casserole.

5. Bake 25 to 30 minutes or until heated through.

Makes 6 servings

Beef Mole Tamale Pie

1½ pounds ground beef

1 medium onion, chopped

1 green bell pepper, chopped

2 cloves garlic, minced

1 package (10 ounces) frozen corn, partially thawed

1¼ cups medium-hot salsa

1 tablespoon unsweetened cocoa powder

2 teaspoons ground cumin

1½ teaspoons salt, divided

1 teaspoon dried oregano

¼ teaspoon ground cinnamon

2 cups (8 ounces) shredded Monterey Jack or Cheddar cheese

⅓ cup chopped fresh cilantro, plus additional for garnish

1 cup all-purpose flour

¾ cup yellow cornmeal

3 tablespoons sugar

2 teaspoons baking powder

⅔ cup milk

3 tablespoons butter, melted

1 egg, beaten

Sour cream (optional)

1. Preheat oven to 400°F. Spray 11×7-inch baking dish with nonstick cooking spray.

2. Brown beef with onion, bell pepper and garlic in large deep skillet over medium heat. Drain fat. Stir in corn, salsa, cocoa, cumin, 1 teaspoon salt, oregano and cinnamon; bring to a boil. Reduce heat to medium-low; cook 8 minutes, stirring occasionally. Remove from heat; stir in cheese and ⅓ cup cilantro. Spread in prepared baking dish.

3. Combine flour, cornmeal, sugar, baking powder and remaining ½ teaspoon salt in large bowl. Add milk, butter and egg; stir just until dry ingredients are moistened. Drop by spoonfuls over beef mixture; spread batter evenly with spatula.

4. Bake 15 minutes. *Reduce oven temperature to 350°F.* Bake 20 minutes or until filling is bubbly and topping is golden brown. Let stand 5 minutes before serving. Garnish with sour cream and additional cilantro.

Makes 6 servings

Breakfast Bake

1 pound ground
   pork sausage

1 teaspoon Italian
   seasoning

½ teaspoon salt

6 eggs

2 cups milk

½ cup CREAM OF WHEAT®
   Hot Cereal (Instant,
   1-minute, 2½-minute
   or 10-minute cook time),
   uncooked

1 teaspoon TRAPPEY'S®
   Red Devil™ Cayenne
   Pepper Sauce

4 cups cubed bread
   stuffing (potato bread
   recommended)

2 cups shredded Cheddar
   cheese

1. Brown sausage in skillet, pressing with fork or spatula to crumble as it cooks. Sprinkle with Italian seasoning and salt; set aside.

2. Combine eggs, milk, Cream of Wheat and pepper sauce in large mixing bowl; mix well. Add cooked sausage and bread stuffing; toss to combine. Pour mixture into 13×9-inch casserole pan; cover. Refrigerate at least 4 hours or overnight.

3. Preheat oven to 350°F. Remove cover and sprinkle cheese over casserole. Cover pan with aluminum foil; bake 30 minutes. Remove foil; bake 15 minutes longer. Serve warm.

Makes 8 servings

Serving Suggestion: Serve this dish with a salad and some fresh fruit on holiday mornings or for a special brunch.

Red, White and Black Bean Casserole

2 tablespoons olive oil

1 yellow or green bell pepper, cut into ½-inch strips

½ cup sliced green onions

1 can (14½ ounces) chunky-style salsa

1 can (4 ounces) diced green chiles, drained

1 package (1¼ ounces) taco seasoning mix

2 tablespoons chopped fresh cilantro

½ teaspoon salt

2 cups cooked rice

1 can (19 ounces) white cannellini beans, rinsed and drained

1 can (about 15 ounces) red kidney beans, rinsed and drained

1 can (about 15 ounces) black beans, rinsed and drained

1 cup (4 ounces) shredded Cheddar cheese, divided

1 package (6-inch) flour tortillas

1. Preheat oven to 350°F. Spray 2- to 3-quart or 13×9-inch baking dish with nonstick cooking spray.

2. Heat oil in large saucepan over medium-high heat. Add bell pepper and green onions; cook and stir about 5 minutes. Add salsa, chiles, taco seasoning, cilantro and salt; cook 5 minutes, stirring occasionally. Stir in rice and beans. Remove from heat; stir in ½ cup cheese. Spoon into prepared baking dish; sprinkle with remaining ½ cup cheese. Cover with foil.

3. Bake 30 to 40 minutes or until heated through. Serve with warm tortillas.

Makes 6 servings

6 Cheese Italian Sausage & Pasta

Prep Time: 20 minutes   **Cook Time:** 25 minutes

1 pound mild or hot Italian sausage

1 large onion, coarsely chopped

2 cloves garlic, minced

1 each large red and green bell peppers, cut into 1-inch squares

1 can (14½ ounces) diced tomatoes or Italian-style tomatoes, undrained

1 can (6 ounces) tomato paste

8 ounces ziti or mostaccioli pasta, cooked and drained

¼ cup chopped fresh basil or 2 teaspoons dried basil

2 cups (8 ounces) SARGENTO® Chef Blends™ Shredded 6 Cheese Italian, divided

1. Discard casings; cut sausage into ½-inch pieces. Cook sausage in large skillet over medium heat 5 minutes or until browned on all sides. Pour off drippings. Add onion, garlic and bell peppers; cook 5 minutes or until sausage is cooked through and vegetables are crisp-tender.

2. Add tomatoes and tomato paste; mix well. Stir in pasta, basil and 1 cup cheese. Transfer to 13×9-inch baking dish. Cover and bake in preheated 375°F oven 20 minutes. Uncover; sprinkle remaining cheese evenly over casserole. Continue to bake 5 minutes or until cheese is melted.

Makes 6 servings

Greek Spinach and Feta Pie

⅓ cup butter, melted

2 eggs

1 container (15 ounces) ricotta cheese

1 package (10 ounces) frozen chopped spinach, thawed and squeezed dry

1 package (4 ounces) crumbled feta cheese

¾ teaspoon finely grated lemon peel

¼ teaspoon black pepper

⅛ teaspoon ground nutmeg

1 package (16 ounces) frozen phyllo dough, thawed

1. Preheat oven to 350°F. Brush 13×9-inch baking dish lightly with some of melted butter.

2. Beat eggs in medium bowl. Add ricotta, spinach, feta, lemon peel, pepper and nutmeg; beat until well blended.

3. Unwrap phyllo dough; remove eight sheets. Cut dough in half crosswise to form 16 rectangles about 13×8½ inches. Cover dough with damp cloth or plastic wrap to prevent drying out while assembling pie. Reserve remaining dough for another use.

4. Place one piece of dough in prepared baking dish; brush lightly with butter. Top with another piece of dough; brush lightly with butter. Continue layering with six pieces of dough, brushing each lightly with butter. Spread spinach mixture evenly over stack of dough.

5. Top spinach mixture with one piece of dough; brush lightly with butter. Repeat layering with remaining seven pieces of dough, brushing each lightly with butter.

6. Bake 35 to 40 minutes or until golden brown.

Makes 6 servings

Sunday Dinner Casserole

- 2 cups egg noodles, cooked and drained
- 2 pounds boneless skinless chicken breasts
- 2 cups sliced sweet onions
- ½ cup dry sherry
- 2 tablespoons sugar
- 2 tablespoons balsamic vinegar
- 1 teaspoon dried thyme
- ½ teaspoon black pepper
- 3 cups chicken broth
- 1 can (about 14 ounces) diced tomatoes
- 2 cloves garlic, minced
- ½ teaspoon red pepper flakes
- ¼ cup chopped fresh basil
- 2 teaspoons grated lemon peel

1. Preheat oven to 400°F. Spread noodles in 13×9-inch baking dish. Top with chicken.

2. Combine onions, sherry, sugar, vinegar, thyme and black pepper in large skillet; cook and stir over medium heat until onions begin to brown. Add broth, tomatoes, garlic and red pepper flakes; mix well. Pour over chicken.

3. Bake 20 minutes. Turn chicken; bake 20 to 25 minutes or until chicken is no longer pink in center. Sprinkle with basil and lemon peel.

Makes 4 to 6 servings

Spinach-Stuffed Turkey Meat Loaf

- 1 sheet (24×12 inches) heavy-duty foil
- 1 pound ground turkey
- 1 cup finely chopped onion
- ½ cup plain dry bread crumbs
- ½ cup finely chopped red bell pepper
- 2 eggs
- 2 tablespoons bacon bits
- 1 teaspoon dried thyme
- ½ teaspoon salt
- ½ teaspoon black pepper
- 1 package (10 ounces) frozen chopped spinach, thawed and squeezed dry
- ⅓ cup sour cream
- ⅓ cup shredded Swiss cheese

1. Preheat oven to 450°F. Center foil over 9×5-inch loaf pan. Gently press foil into pan; leaving 1-inch overhang on sides of pan and 5-inch overhang on each end. Generously spray foil with nonstick cooking spray.

2. Combine turkey, onion, bread crumbs, bell pepper, eggs, bacon bits, thyme, salt and black pepper in medium bowl; mix well. Place about 3 cups mixture in prepared pan, packing down lightly and making indentation, end to end, with back of large spoon.

3. Combine spinach, sour cream and cheese in small bowl; mix well. Spoon into indentation. Cover with remaining turkey mixture, packing down lightly. Fold foil over sides to cover completely; crimp foil, leaving head space for heat circulation.

4. Bake about 50 minutes or until cooked through. Let stand, covered, 10 minutes before serving. Cut into 1-inch slices.

Makes 8 servings

Ratatouille Pot Pie

¼ cup olive oil

1 medium eggplant (about 1 pound), peeled and cut into ½-inch pieces

1 large onion, chopped

1 green or yellow bell pepper, chopped

1½ teaspoons minced garlic

1 can (about 14 ounces) diced tomatoes with garlic and herbs or Italian stewed tomatoes, undrained

1 teaspoon dried basil

½ teaspoon red pepper flakes

¼ teaspoon salt

1 tablespoon balsamic vinegar

2 cups (8 ounces) shredded mozzarella cheese, divided

1 package (about 10 ounces) refrigerated pizza dough

1. Preheat oven to 425°F.

2. Heat oil in large skillet over medium heat. Add eggplant, onion, bell pepper and garlic; cook 10 minutes or until eggplant begins to brown, stirring occasionally. Add tomatoes, basil, red pepper flakes and salt; cook over medium-low heat 5 minutes, stirring occasionally. Remove from heat; stir in vinegar. Let stand 10 minutes. Stir in 1 cup cheese.

3. Spoon mixture into 11×7-inch baking dish; sprinkle with remaining 1 cup cheese. Unroll pizza dough; make decorative cut-outs with small cookie cutter, if desired. Place dough over vegetable mixture; spray with nonstick cooking spray.

4. Bake 15 minutes or until filling is bubbly and crust is golden brown. Let stand 5 minutes before serving.

Makes 6 servings

Easy Chicken Chalupas

1 rotisserie chicken
(about 2 pounds)

8 (8-inch) flour tortillas

2 cups (8 ounces) shredded
Cheddar cheese

1 cup mild green salsa

1 cup mild red salsa

1. Preheat oven to 350°F. Spray 13×9-inch baking dish with nonstick cooking spray.

2. Shred chicken; discard skin and bones. Place two tortillas in prepared baking dish, overlapping slightly. Layer tortillas with 1 cup chicken, ½ cup cheese and ¼ cup of each salsa. Repeat layers three times.

3. Bake 25 minutes or until bubbly and heated through.

Makes 6 servings

Tip: Serve with toppings such as sour cream, chopped fresh cilantro, sliced black olives, sliced green onions and sliced or diced avocado.

Spicy Sausage Popover Pizza

Prep Time: 15 minutes   **Bake Time:** 21 to 23 minutes

8 ounces turkey breakfast sausage patties, crumbled

8 ounces ground turkey

⅓ cup chopped onion

1 clove garlic, minced

¾ cup chopped red bell pepper

1½ cups all-purpose flour

¼ teaspoon salt

¼ teaspoon red pepper flakes

1 cup milk

3 eggs

1 cup (4 ounces) shredded Cheddar cheese

½ cup (2 ounces) shredded mozzarella cheese

Pizza sauce, heated

1. Preheat oven to 425°F. Generously spray 13×9-inch baking dish with nonstick cooking spray.

2. Combine sausage, ground turkey, onion and garlic in large skillet; cook and stir over medium heat until turkey is browned. Drain fat. Stir in bell pepper.

3. Combine flour, salt and red pepper flakes in large bowl. Beat milk and eggs in medium bowl until well blended. Add to flour mixture; whisk until smooth. Pour into prepared baking dish. Top with sausage mixture; sprinkle with Cheddar and mozzarella.

4. Bake 21 to 23 minutes or until puffed and golden brown. Serve with pizza sauce

Makes 8 servings

Chicken Zucchini Casserole

1 package (about 6 ounces) herb-flavored stuffing mix

½ cup (1 stick) butter, melted

2 cups cubed zucchini

1½ cups chopped cooked chicken

1 can (10¾ ounces) condensed cream of celery soup, undiluted

1 cup grated carrots

1 onion, chopped

½ cup sour cream

½ cup (2 ounces) shredded Cheddar cheese

1. Preheat oven to 350°F. Combine stuffing mix and butter in medium bowl; mix well. Reserve 1 cup stuffing; spread remaining stuffing in 13×9-inch baking dish.

2. Combine zucchini, chicken, soup, carrots, onion and sour cream in large bowl; mix well. Pour over stuffing in baking dish; top with reserved 1 cup stuffing and cheese.

3. Bake 40 to 45 minutes or until heated through.

Makes 8 servings

Ham and Cheese Bread Pudding

1 small loaf (8 ounces) sourdough, country French or Italian bread, cut into 1-inch-thick slices

3 tablespoons butter, softened

8 ounces ham or smoked ham, cut into ½-inch pieces

1 cup (4 ounces) shredded Cheddar cheese

3 eggs

2 cups milk

1 teaspoon ground mustard

½ teaspoon salt

⅛ teaspoon white pepper

1. Spray 11×7-inch baking dish with nonstick cooking spray.

2. Spread one side of each bread slice with butter. Cut into 1-inch cubes; place on bottom of prepared baking dish. Top with ham; sprinkle with cheese.

3. Beat eggs in medium bowl. Beat in milk, mustard, salt and pepper until well blended. Pour egg mixture over bread mixture in baking dish; cover and refrigerate at least 6 hours or overnight.

4. Preheat oven to 350°F. Bake, uncovered, 45 to 50 minutes or until puffed and golden brown and knife inserted into center comes out clean. Garnish as desired. Serve immediately.

Makes 8 servings

Creamy Chicken Enchiladas

Prep Time: 20 minutes   **Bake Time:** 40 minutes

1 can (10¾ ounces) CAMPBELL'S® Condensed Cream of Chicken Soup (Regular or 98% Fat Free)

1 container (8 ounces) sour cream

1 cup PACE® Picante Sauce

2 teaspoons chili powder

2 cups chopped cooked chicken

1 cup shredded Monterey Jack cheese (4 ounces)

12 flour tortillas (8-inch), warmed

1 medium tomato, chopped (about 1 cup)

1 green onion, sliced (about 2 tablespoons)

1. Mix the soup, sour cream, picante sauce and chili powder in a small bowl.

2. Stir **1 cup** of the soup mixture, chicken and cheese in a medium bowl.

3. Spoon about ¼ **cup** of the chicken mixture down the center of each tortilla. Roll up the tortillas and place them seam-side down in 13×9-inch (3-quart) shallow baking dish. Pour the remaining soup mixture over the filled tortillas. **Cover.**

4. Bake at 350°F. for 40 minutes or until hot and bubbly. Top with the tomato and green onion.

Makes 6 servings

Kitchen Tip: For **2 cups** chopped cooked chicken, cook **1 pound** skinless, boneless chicken breasts or thighs, cubed, in medium saucepan over medium heat in **4 cups** boiling water, 5 minutes or until chicken is no longer pink. Drain and chop chicken.

Italian Tomato-Braised Lamb

4 bone-in lamb shoulder chops (about 1 inch thick, about 2½ pounds total)

Salt and black pepper

2 onions, cut into quarters and thinly sliced

1 can (28 ounces) whole plum tomatoes, undrained

2 tablespoons olive oil

2 tablespoons red wine vinegar

3 cloves garlic, minced

1½ teaspoons dried oregano

3 to 4 sprigs fresh rosemary

Hot cooked polenta or pasta (optional)

1. Preheat oven to 400°F. Place lamb chops in 13×9-inch baking dish; season with salt and pepper. Top with onions.

2. Pour tomatoes with juice into medium bowl; break up tomatoes. Stir in oil, vinegar, garlic and oregano; mix well. Pour mixture over lamb and onions. Tuck rosemary sprigs into tomato mixture. Cover with foil.

3. Bake 45 minutes. Turn lamb; bake, uncovered, 1 hour and 15 minutes or until lamb is tender. Remove and discard rosemary sprigs. Serve with polenta, if desired.

Makes 4 servings

Hash Brown Casserole with Bacon

1 package (32 ounces) frozen Southern-style hash brown potatoes, thawed

2 cups sour cream

1 can (10¾ ounces) condensed cream of chicken soup, undiluted

1½ cups (6 ounces) shredded sharp Cheddar cheese

¾ cup thinly sliced green onions

4 slices bacon, crisp-cooked and crumbled

2 teaspoons hot pepper sauce

¼ teaspoon garlic salt

1. Preheat oven to 350°F. Spray 13×9-inch baking pan with nonstick cooking spray.

2. Combine potatoes, sour cream, soup, cheese, green onions, bacon, hot pepper sauce and garlic salt in large bowl; mix well. Spoon into prepared baking dish.

3. Bake 55 to 60 minutes or until potatoes are tender and cooked through. Stir before serving.

Makes 12 servings

Cheddar and Leek Strata

8 eggs

2 cups milk

½ cup porter or stout

2 cloves garlic, minced

¼ teaspoon salt

¼ teaspoon black pepper

1 loaf (16 ounces) sourdough bread, cut into ½-inch cubes

2 small leeks, coarsely chopped

1 red bell pepper, chopped

1½ cups (6 ounces) shredded Swiss cheese

1½ cups (6 ounces) shredded sharp Cheddar cheese

1. Spray 13×9-inch baking dish with nonstick cooking spray.

2. Beat eggs, milk, porter, garlic, salt and black pepper in large bowl until well blended. Spread half of bread cubes in prepared baking dish; sprinkle with half of leeks and half of bell pepper. Top with ¾ cup Swiss cheese and ¾ cup Cheddar cheese. Repeat layers. Pour egg mixture evenly over top.

3. Cover tightly with plastic wrap or foil. Weigh down top of strata with slightly smaller baking dish. Refrigerate at least 2 hours or overnight.

4. Preheat oven to 350°F. Bake, uncovered, 40 to 45 minutes or until center is set. Serve immediately.

Makes 12 servings

Taco Casserole Supreme

Prep Time: 20 minutes   **Cook Time:** 35 minutes

REYNOLDS WRAP®
Non-Stick Foil

2 pounds lean ground beef

1 large onion, chopped

1 large green bell pepper,
chopped

2 packages (1¼ ounces *each*)
taco seasoning mix

1 cup water

1 package (16 ounces)
frozen whole kernel corn

1 jar (24 ounces) chunky
salsa, divided

1 package (8 ounces)
shredded sharp Cheddar
cheese, divided

PREHEAT oven to 350°F. Line a 13×9×2-inch baking pan with REYNOLDS WRAP®
Non-Stick Foil with non-stick (dull) side toward food; set aside.

BROWN ground beef, onion and pepper in a large skillet, over medium-high heat; drain.
Stir in taco seasoning mix and water. Stir in corn; bring to a boil. Reduce heat and simmer
10 minutes. Spoon half of mixture in bottom of foil-lined pan. Top with 1 cup salsa and
1 cup cheese. Top with remaining meat mixture and salsa.

BAKE 30 to 35 minutes or until bubbly. Sprinkle with remaining cheese; let stand 5 minutes.
Serve with tortilla chips, if desired.

Makes 8 to 12 servings

Sheet Pan Meals

Honey Lemon Garlic Chicken

- 2 lemons, divided
- 2 tablespoons butter, melted
- 2 tablespoons honey
- 3 cloves garlic, chopped
- 2 sprigs fresh rosemary, leaves removed from stems
- 1 teaspoon coarse salt
- ½ teaspoon black pepper
- 3 pounds chicken (4 bone-in skin-on chicken thighs and 4 drumsticks)
- 1¼ pounds potatoes, cut into halves or quarters

1. Preheat oven to 375°F. Line baking sheet with parchment paper, if desired.

2. Grate peel and squeeze juice from one lemon. Cut remaining lemon into slices.

3. Combine lemon peel, lemon juice, butter, honey, garlic, rosemary leaves, salt and pepper in small bowl; mix well. Combine chicken, potatoes and lemon slices in large bowl. Pour butter mixture over chicken and potatoes; toss to coat. Arrange in single layer on baking sheet.

4. Bake about 1 hour or until potatoes are tender and chicken is cooked through (165°F). Cover loosely with foil if chicken skin is becoming too dark.

Makes 4 servings

Beef Tenderloin with Roasted Vegetables

1 beef tenderloin roast (about 3 pounds), trimmed

½ cup chardonnay or other dry white wine

½ cup reduced-sodium soy sauce

2 cloves garlic, sliced

1 tablespoon fresh rosemary leaves

1 tablespoon Dijon mustard

1 teaspoon dry mustard

1 pound small red or white potatoes, cut into 1-inch pieces

1 pound brussels sprouts

1 package (12 ounces) baby carrots

1. Place beef in large resealable food storage bag. Combine wine, soy sauce, garlic, rosemary, Dijon mustard and dry mustard in small bowl; pour over beef. Seal bag; turn to coat. Marinate in refrigerator 4 to 12 hours, turning several times.

2. Preheat oven to 425°F. Spray baking sheet with nonstick cooking spray.

3. Combine potatoes, brussels sprouts and carrots on prepared baking sheet. Remove roast from marinade. Pour marinade over vegetables; toss to coat. Spread vegetables in single layer. Cover with foil; roast 30 minutes.

4. Stir vegetables; arrange beef on top. Roast, uncovered, 35 to 45 minutes or until beef is 135°F for medium rare or to desired doneness. Remove beef to cutting board; tent with foil. Let stand 10 to 15 minutes before slicing. (Internal temperature will continue to rise 5° to 10°F during stand time.) Reserve drippings from baking sheet to make gravy, if desired.

5. Slice beef; arrange on serving platter with roasted vegetables.

Makes 10 servings

Oven-Roasted Boston Scrod

- 3 tablespoons all-purpose flour
- ½ cup seasoned dry bread crumbs
- 1 teaspoon grated lemon peel
- 1 teaspoon paprika
- 1 teaspoon dried dill weed
- 2 egg whites
- 1 tablespoon water
- 1½ pounds Boston scrod or orange roughy fillets, cut into 6 pieces (4 ounces each)
- 2 tablespoons butter, melted
- Tartar Sauce (recipe follows)
- Lemon wedges

1. Preheat oven to 400°F. Spray baking sheet with nonstick cooking spray. Place flour in shallow bowl. Combine bread crumbs, lemon peel, paprika and dill weed in another shallow bowl; mix well. Beat egg whites and water in third shallow bowl until blended.

2. Working with one piece of fish at a time, coat with flour mixture, shaking off excess. Dip in egg white mixture, letting excess drip off. Roll in bread crumb mixture to coat. Place on prepared baking sheet; drizzle with butter.

3. Roast 15 to 18 minutes or until fish begins to flake when tested with fork.

4. Meanwhile, prepare Tartar Sauce. Serve fish with Tartar Sauce and lemon wedges.

Makes 6 servings

Tartar Sauce

- ½ cup mayonnaise
- ¼ cup sweet pickle relish
- 2 teaspoons Dijon mustard
- ¼ teaspoon hot pepper sauce (optional)

Combine mayonnaise, pickle relish, mustard and hot pepper sauce, if desired, in small bowl; mix well.

Makes ⅔ cup

Roast Chicken and Potatoes Catalan

2 tablespoons olive oil

2 tablespoons lemon juice

1 teaspoon dried thyme

½ teaspoon salt

¼ teaspoon ground red pepper

¼ teaspoon ground saffron *or* ½ teaspoon crushed saffron threads or turmeric

2 large baking potatoes (about 1½ pounds), cut into 1½-inch pieces

4 bone-in chicken breasts (about 2 pounds), skin removed

1 cup sliced red bell pepper

1 cup frozen peas, thawed

Lemon wedges

1. Preheat oven to 400°F. Spray baking sheet with nonstick cooking spray.

2. Combine oil, lemon juice, thyme, salt, ground red pepper and saffron in large bowl; mix well. Add potatoes; toss to coat.

3. Arrange potatoes in single layer around edges of baking sheet. Place chicken in center of baking sheet; brush both sides of chicken with remaining oil mixture in bowl.

4. Roast 20 minutes. Turn potatoes; baste chicken with pan juices. Add bell pepper; roast 20 minutes or until chicken is cooked through (165°F) and potatoes are browned. Stir peas into potato mixture; roast 5 minutes or until heated through. Garnish with lemon wedges.

Makes 4 servings

Roasted Salmon with Horseradish Rosemary Aioli

4 salmon fillets (6 ounces each), rinsed and patted dry

1 tablespoon extra virgin olive oil

½ teaspoon salt

½ teaspoon coarsely ground black pepper

½ cup mayonnaise

¼ cup sour cream

2 to 3 teaspoons prepared horseradish

1 teaspoon Dijon mustard

½ teaspoon minced garlic

¼ teaspoon dried rosemary

1. Preheat oven to 400°F. Line baking sheet with heavy-duty foil; spray lightly with nonstick cooking spray.

2. Rub both sides of salmon with oil; sprinkle with salt and pepper. Press seasonings to adhere. Place fish on prepared baking sheet.

3. Roast 12 minutes or until center is opaque.

4. Meanwhile, prepare aioli. Combine mayonnaise, sour cream, horseradish, mustard, garlic and rosemary in small bowl; mix well. Serve with fish.

Makes 4 servings

Note: The sauce may be made up to 1 week in advance. Cover and store in refrigerator.

BBQ Chicken Stromboli

1 **rotisserie chicken***
(2 to 2¼ pounds)

⅓ **cup barbecue sauce**

1 **package (about 14 ounces)
refrigerated pizza dough**

1 **cup (4 ounces) shredded
Cheddar cheese**

⅓ **cup sliced green onions,
divided**

*If desired, substitute 8 ounces roast chicken breast from the deli, chopped, for the shredded rotisserie chicken.

1. Shred chicken with forks; discard skin and bones. (You should have about 4 cups shredded chicken.)

2. Combine 2 cups chicken and barbecue sauce in medium bowl; mix well. Cover and refrigerate or freeze remaining chicken for another use.

3. Preheat oven to 400°F. Line baking sheet with parchment paper or spray lightly with nonstick cooking spray. Unroll pizza dough on baking sheet; pat into 12×9-inch rectangle.

4. Spread chicken mixture lengthwise down center of dough, leaving 2½ inches on each side. Sprinkle with cheese and ¼ cup green onions. Fold long sides of dough over filling; press edges to seal. Sprinkle with remaining green onions.

5. Bake 19 to 22 minutes or until golden brown. Let stand 10 minutes before slicing.

Makes 6 servings

Rosemary Roast Pork Tenderloin and Vegetables

¼ cup reduced-sodium
   chicken broth

1 tablespoon olive or
   vegetable oil

3 large parsnips, peeled
   and cut diagonally
   into ½-inch slices

2 cups baby carrots

1 red bell pepper, cut
   into ¾-inch pieces

1 sweet or yellow onion,
   cut into wedges

2 small pork tenderloins
   (12 ounces each)

2 tablespoons Dijon
   mustard

2 teaspoons dried rosemary

1 teaspoon salt

½ teaspoon black pepper

1. Preheat oven to 400°F. Spray baking sheet with nonstick cooking spray.

2. Combine broth and oil in small bowl. Combine parsnips, carrots and 3 tablespoons broth mixture on prepared baking sheet; toss to coat. Spread vegetables in single layer.

3. Roast 10 minutes. Add bell pepper, onion and remaining broth mixture to baking sheet; toss to coat. Push vegetables to edges of pan. Place pork in center of pan; spread with mustard. Sprinkle pork and vegetables with rosemary, salt and black pepper.

4. Roast 25 to 30 minutes or until vegetables are tender and pork is 145°F. Remove pork to cutting board; tent with foil and let stand 5 minutes. Cut into ½-inch slices; serve with vegetables and any juices from pan.

Makes 6 servings

Mexican Pizza

1 package (about 14 ounces) refrigerated pizza dough

1 cup chunky salsa

1 teaspoon ground cumin

1 cup canned black beans, rinsed and drained*

1 cup frozen corn, thawed

½ cup sliced green onions

1½ cups (6 ounces) shredded Mexican cheese blend

½ cup chopped fresh cilantro

*Save the remaining ¾ cup beans (from a 15- or 16-ounce can) in the refrigerator for up to 4 days to use in soups or salads.

1. Preheat oven to 425°F. Spray 15×10-inch baking sheet with nonstick cooking spray.

2. Unroll pizza dough on prepared baking sheet; press dough to edges of pan. Bake 8 minutes.

3. Combine salsa and cumin in small bowl; spread over partially baked crust. Top with beans, corn and green onions.

4. Bake 8 minutes or until crust is deep golden brown. Sprinkle with cheese; bake 2 minutes or until cheese is melted. Sprinkle with cilantro.

Makes 8 servings

Oven-Fried Chicken Cutlets

1⅓ cups light-colored beer, such as pale ale

2 tablespoons buttermilk

1¼ cups panko bread crumbs*

½ cup grated Parmesan cheese

4 chicken breast cutlets (about 1¼ pounds)

½ teaspoon salt

¼ teaspoon black pepper

*Panko bread crumbs are Japanese bread crumbs that are much lighter and less dense than ones often used in America. Panko bread crumbs can be found in Asian markets or in the Asian foods section of your supermarket.

1. Preheat oven to 400°F. Line large baking sheet with foil.

2. Combine beer and buttermilk in shallow bowl; mix well. Combine panko and Parmesan in another shallow bowl.

3. Sprinkle chicken with salt and pepper. Dip in beer mixture; roll in panko mixture to coat. Place on prepared baking sheet.

4. Bake 25 to 30 minutes or until no longer pink in center.

Makes 4 servings

Serving Suggestion: Serve this crispy chicken with short-cut baked potatoes. Before preparing the chicken, partially cook whole russet potatoes (scrub and pierce them with a fork or knife several times) in the microwave on HIGH 5 minutes or just until they begin to soften. Place the partially cooked potatoes on the baking sheet with the chicken; both the baked potatoes and the chicken should be done about the same time.

Garlic Pork with Roasted Red Potatoes

½ teaspoon paprika

½ teaspoon garlic powder

1 pork tenderloin
(about 1 pound)

1½ tablespoons olive oil,
divided

8 to 10 new potatoes,
scrubbed and quartered
(about 1 pound)

1 teaspoon dried oregano

½ teaspoon salt

½ teaspoon black pepper

1. Preheat oven to 425°F. Spray baking sheet with nonstick cooking spray.

2. Combine paprika and garlic powder in small bowl; sprinkle over pork.

3. Heat ½ tablespoon oil in large skillet over medium-high heat. Add pork; cook 3 minutes per side or until browned. Place in center of prepared baking sheet.

4. Remove skillet from heat. Add remaining 1 tablespoon oil, potatoes and oregano; stir to coat potatoes, scraping up browned bits from bottom of skillet. Arrange potato mixture around pork. Combine salt and pepper in small bowl; sprinkle over pork and vegetables.

5. Roast 22 minutes or until pork is 145°F. Remove pork to cutting board; let stand 5 minutes before slicing. Stir potatoes; cover loosely with foil until ready to serve.

Makes 4 servings

Drunken Roast Chicken

1 whole chicken (3 to 3½ pounds), quartered

¼ cup soy sauce

4 tablespoons dry sherry, divided

4 cloves garlic, minced

1 tablespoon minced fresh ginger

½ teaspoon red pepper flakes

½ cup plum sauce

2 teaspoons Chinese hot mustard

1. Place chicken quarters in large resealable food storage bag. Combine soy sauce, 3 tablespoons sherry, garlic, ginger and red pepper flakes in small bowl; pour over chicken. Seal bag; turn to coat. Marinate chicken in refrigerator at least 30 minutes or up to 4 hours.

2. Combine plum sauce, mustard and remaining 1 tablespoon sherry in small bowl; set aside.

3. Preheat oven to 375°F. Line baking sheet with foil. Remove chicken from bag, reserving marinade. Place chicken on prepared baking sheet.

4. Roast 25 minutes. Brush reserved marinade over chicken; discard any remaining marinade. *Increase oven temperature to 450°F;* roast 20 minutes or until cooked through (165°F). Serve chicken with plum sauce mixture.

Makes 4 servings

Wild Mushroom Flatbread

1 package (about 14 ounces) refrigerated pizza dough

1 tablespoon olive oil

1 package (4 ounces) sliced cremini mushrooms

1 package (4 ounces) sliced shiitake mushrooms

1 shallot, thinly sliced

2 cloves garlic, minced

½ teaspoon salt

¾ cup (3 ounces) grated Gruyère cheese

2 teaspoons chopped fresh thyme

1. Preheat oven to 400°F. Line baking sheet with parchment paper. Spray with nonstick cooking spray.

2. Roll out pizza dough into 15×10-inch rectangle on lightly floured surface. Place on prepared baking sheet. Bake 10 minutes.

3. Meanwhile, heat oil in large nonstick skillet over medium-high heat. Add mushrooms; cook and stir 5 minutes. Add shallot and garlic; cook and stir 5 minutes or until tender. Season with salt.

4. Arrange mushroom mixture evenly over partially baked crust. Sprinkle with cheese and thyme.

5. Bake 8 minutes or until cheese is melted.

Makes about 8 servings

Jalapeño-Lime Chicken

8 bone-in chicken thighs

3 tablespoons jalapeño jelly

1 tablespoon olive oil

1 tablespoon lime juice

1 clove garlic, minced

1 teaspoon chili powder

½ teaspoon black pepper

⅛ teaspoon salt

1. Preheat oven to 400°F. Line baking sheet with foil; spray with nonstick cooking spray.

2. Arrange chicken in single layer on prepared baking sheet.

3. Bake 15 minutes; drain off juices. Combine jelly, oil, lime juice, garlic, chili powder, pepper and salt in small bowl; mix well. Turn chicken; brush with half of jelly mixture. Bake 20 minutes. Turn chicken; brush with remaining jelly mixture. Bake 10 to 15 minutes or until cooked through (165°F).

Makes 8 servings

Roasted Dijon Lamb with Herbs and Country Vegetables

20 cloves garlic, peeled
(about 2 medium heads)

¼ cup Dijon mustard

2 tablespoons water

2 tablespoons fresh
rosemary leaves

1 tablespoon fresh thyme

1¼ teaspoons salt, divided

1 teaspoon black pepper

4½ pounds boneless leg of
lamb,* trimmed

1 pound parsnips, cut
diagonally into
½-inch pieces

1 pound carrots, cut
diagonally into
½-inch pieces

2 large onions, cut into
½-inch wedges

3 tablespoons extra virgin
olive oil, divided

*If unavailable, substitute packaged
marinated lamb and rinse it off.

1. Combine garlic, mustard, water, rosemary, thyme, ¾ teaspoon salt and pepper in food processor; process until smooth. Spread mixture over top and sides of lamb. Cover and refrigerate at least 8 hours.

2. Preheat oven to 500°F. Line baking sheet with foil; top with broiler rack. Spray rack with nonstick cooking spray.

3. Combine parsnips, carrots, onions and 2 tablespoons oil in large bowl; toss to coat. Spread evenly on rack; top with lamb.

4. Roast 15 minutes. *Reduce oven temperature to 325°F.* Roast 1 hour 20 minutes or until 155°F for medium or to desired doneness. Remove lamb to cutting board; let stand 10 minutes before slicing. Continue roasting vegetables 10 minutes.

5. Transfer vegetables to large bowl. Add remaining 1 tablespoon oil and ½ teaspoon salt; toss to coat. Thinly slice lamb and serve with vegetables.

Makes 8 to 10 servings

Roasted Dill Scrod with Asparagus

1 bunch asparagus spears (12 ounces), ends trimmed

1 tablespoon olive oil

4 scrod or cod fillets (about 5 ounces each)

1 tablespoon lemon juice

1 teaspoon dried dill weed

½ teaspoon salt

¼ teaspoon black pepper

Paprika (optional)

1. Preheat oven to 425°F.

2. Place asparagus on baking sheet; drizzle with oil. Roll asparagus to coat lightly with oil. Push to edges of baking sheet, stacking asparagus into two layers.

3. Arrange scrod in center of baking sheet; drizzle with lemon juice. Combine dill weed, salt and pepper in small bowl; sprinkle over fish and asparagus. Sprinkle with paprika, if desired.

4. Roast 15 to 17 minutes or until asparagus is crisp-tender and fish begins to flake when tested with fork.

Makes 4 servings

Caprese Pizza

1 loaf (1 pound) frozen pizza or bread dough, thawed

1 container (12 ounces) bruschetta sauce

1 container (8 ounces) pearl-size fresh mozzarella cheese (perlini), drained*

*If pearl-size mozzarella is not available, use one (8-ounce) ball of fresh mozzarella and chop into $1/4$-inch pieces.

1. Preheat oven to 400°F. Spray baking sheet with nonstick cooking spray.

2. Roll out pizza dough into 15×10-inch rectangle on lightly floured surface. Place on prepared baking sheet. Cover loosely with plastic wrap; let rest 10 minutes. Meanwhile, place bruschetta sauce in colander; let drain 10 minutes.

3. Prick surface of dough several times with fork. Bake 10 minutes.

4. Sprinkle with drained bruschetta sauce; top with mozzarella. Bake 10 minutes or until cheese is melted and crust is golden brown. Serve warm.

Makes 6 servings

Note: Bruschetta sauce is a mixture of diced fresh tomatoes, garlic, basil and olive oil. It is typically found in the refrigerated section of the supermarket with other prepared dips such as hummus.

Dutch Oven Delights

Chicken Cassoulet

- 4 slices bacon
- ¼ cup all-purpose flour
  Salt and black pepper
- 1¾ pounds bone-in chicken pieces
- 2 chicken sausages (2¼ ounces each), cut into ¼-inch slices
- 1 medium onion, chopped
- 1½ cups diced red and green bell peppers
- 2 cloves garlic, minced
- 1 teaspoon dried thyme
- 1 teaspoon olive oil
- ½ cup dry white wine or chicken broth
- 2 cans (about 15 ounces each) cannellini or Great Northern beans, rinsed and drained

1. Preheat oven to 350°F. Cook bacon in Dutch oven over medium-high heat until crisp; drain on paper towel-lined plate. Cut into 1-inch pieces. Drain all but 2 tablespoons drippings from pan.

2. Place flour in shallow bowl; season with salt and black pepper. Dip chicken pieces in flour mixture, shaking off excess. Brown chicken in batches in Dutch oven over medium-high heat; remove to plate. Lightly brown sausages in Dutch oven; remove to plate.

3. Add onion, bell peppers, garlic and thyme to Dutch oven; cook and stir over medium heat 5 minutes or until softened, adding oil as needed to prevent sticking. Add wine; cook and stir over medium heat, scraping up browned bits from bottom of pan. Add beans; mix well. Top with chicken, sausages and bacon.

4. Cover and bake 40 minutes. Remove cover; bake 15 minutes or until chicken is cooked through (165°F).

Makes 6 servings

Pozole

1 large onion, thinly sliced

1 tablespoon olive oil

2 teaspoons dried oregano

1 clove garlic, minced

½ teaspoon ground cumin

2 cans (about 14 ounces each) chicken broth

1 package (10 ounces) frozen corn*

2 cans (4 ounces each) diced green chiles, undrained

1 can (2¼ ounces) sliced black olives, drained

12 ounces boneless skinless chicken breasts, cut into thin strips

Chopped fresh cilantro (optional)

*For a more authentic flavor, substitute 1 can (about 15 ounces) yellow hominy, drained, for the frozen corn.

1. Combine onion, oil, oregano, garlic and cumin in Dutch oven; cover and cook over low heat about 6 minutes or until onion is tender, stirring occasionally.

2. Stir in broth, corn, chiles and olives; cover and bring to a boil over high heat.

3. Stir in chicken. Reduce heat to medium-low; cover and cook about 4 minutes or until chicken is no longer pink. Garnish with cilantro.

Makes 6 servings

Seafood Niçoise

2 tablespoons olive oil

1 leek, white part only, sliced (1 cup)

2 shallots, chopped

6 to 8 small red potatoes, cut into quarters

1 can (15 ounces) tomato purée

1 to 1½ cups bottled clam juice, divided

1 teaspoon salt

1 teaspoon herbes de Provence*

¼ teaspoon dried tarragon

1 pound sea scallops or tuna, cut into 1-inch pieces

½ cup sliced pitted black olives

½ cup frozen French-cut string beans (optional)

*Or substitute ¼ teaspoon *each* rubbed sage, dried rosemary, dried thyme, dried oregano, dried marjoram and dried basil.

1. Heat oil in Dutch oven over medium-high heat. Add leek and shallots; cook and stir until leek is soft. Add potatoes; cook 10 minutes, stirring occasionally.

2. Stir in tomato purée, 1 cup clam juice, salt, herbes de Provence and tarragon; bring to a boil over high heat. Reduce heat to low; cover and simmer 40 minutes or until potatoes are fork-tender.

3. If sauce is too thick, add remaining ½ cup clam juice. Add scallops, olives and beans, if desired; cover and simmer 5 to 6 minutes or until scallops are opaque.

Makes 4 servings

Italian-Style Bean Soup

1½ cups dried Great
    Northern or navy beans,
    rinsed and sorted

5 cups water

1 cup pasta sauce

1 tablespoon minced onion

2 teaspoons dried basil

2 cubes chicken bouillon

1 teaspoon dried parsley
   flakes

½ teaspoon minced garlic

1½ cups uncooked medium
    pasta shells

Salt and black pepper

¼ cup grated Parmesan
   cheese

1. Place beans in large bowl; cover with water. Soak 6 to 8 hours or overnight.*

2. Drain beans; discard water. Combine soaked beans, 5 cups water, pasta sauce, onion, basil, bouillon, parsley flakes and garlic in Dutch oven; bring to a boil over high heat. Reduce heat to low; cover and simmer 2 to 2½ hours or until beans are tender.

3. Stir in pasta; cover and simmer about 15 minutes or until pasta is tender. Season with salt and pepper. Sprinkle with cheese.

To quick-soak beans, place in large saucepan; cover with water. Bring to a boil over high heat; boil 2 minutes. Remove from heat; cover and let stand 1 hour.

Makes 8 to 10 servings

Variations: Add 8 ounces baby spinach, 8 slices crumbled crisp-cooked bacon, or 1 package (15 ounces) frozen precooked Italian style meatballs, not in sauce.

Corned Beef and Cabbage

3½ to 4 pounds packaged
    corned beef brisket

3 carrots, cut into
    1½-inch pieces

2 small onions, quartered

3 stalks celery, cut into
    1½-inch pieces

1 bunch fresh parsley

2 large sprigs fresh thyme

1 head green cabbage
    (about 2 pounds),
    cut into 8 wedges

1½ pounds small red
    potatoes

1 cup sour cream

2 tablespoons prepared
    horseradish

½ teaspoon coarse salt

Chopped fresh parsley
    (optional)

1. Combine corned beef, carrots, onions and celery in Dutch oven. Tie parsley and thyme together with kitchen string; add to Dutch oven. Add water to cover beef by 1 inch; bring to a boil over high heat. Reduce heat to medium-low; cover and cook about 2½ hours or until beef is almost tender.

2. Add cabbage and potatoes; cover and cook about 30 minutes or until beef, cabbage and potatoes are tender.

3. Meanwhile, combine sour cream, horseradish and ½ teaspoon salt in medium bowl; mix well. Refrigerate until ready to serve.

4. Remove herbs from Dutch oven and discard. Remove beef to cutting board; let stand 10 minutes. Slice beef across the grain. Arrange on serving platter with vegetables; season vegetables with additional salt to taste. Sprinkle with chopped parsley, if desired; serve with horseradish sauce.

Makes 8 servings

Four-Bean Chili Stew

2 tablespoons vegetable oil

1 onion, coarsely chopped

3 cloves garlic, chopped

1 zucchini, halved lengthwise and thinly sliced

½ red bell pepper, chopped

2 cans (11 ounces each) tomatillos,* drained

1 can (about 15 ounces) red kidney beans, rinsed and drained

1 can (about 15 ounces) black beans, rinsed and drained

1 can (about 15 ounces) Great Northern beans, rinsed and drained

1 can (about 15 ounces) chickpeas, rinsed and drained

1 can (15 ounces) tomato sauce

½ cup barbecue sauce

1½ teaspoons ground cumin

1 to 1½ teaspoons chili powder

½ teaspoon salt

¼ to ½ teaspoon ground red pepper

Sour cream, chopped tomato, chopped onion and shredded Cheddar cheese (optional)

Flour tortillas, warmed (optional)

Chopped fresh cilantro (optional)

*Tomatillos can be found in Mexican grocery stores or in the specialty food section of large supermarkets.

1. Heat oil in Dutch oven over medium-high heat. Add onion and garlic; cook and stir until onion is soft. Add zucchini and bell pepper; cook and stir 5 minutes.

2. Add tomatillos, beans, chickpeas, tomato sauce, barbecue sauce, cumin, chili powder, salt and ground red pepper; bring to a boil over high heat. Reduce heat to low; cover and simmer 30 minutes.

3. Serve with desired toppings and tortillas. Garnish with cilantro.

Makes 4 to 6 servings

Cider Pork and Onions

2 to 3 tablespoons vegetable oil

4 to 4½ pounds bone-in pork shoulder roast (pork butt)

4 to 5 medium onions, sliced (about 4 cups)

1 teaspoon salt, divided

4 cloves garlic, minced

3 sprigs fresh rosemary

½ teaspoon black pepper

2 to 3 cups apple cider

1. Preheat oven to 325°F. Heat 2 tablespoons oil in Dutch oven over medium-high heat. Add pork; cook until browned on all sides. Remove to plate.

2. Add onions and ½ teaspoon salt to Dutch oven; cook and stir 10 minutes or until translucent, adding additional oil as needed to prevent scorching. Add garlic; cook and stir 1 minute. Add pork and rosemary; sprinkle with remaining ½ teaspoon salt and pepper. Add cider to come about halfway up sides of pork.

3. Cover and bake 2 to 2½ hours or until very tender. (Meat should be almost falling off bones.) Remove to large platter and keep warm.

4. Remove rosemary sprigs from Dutch oven. Boil liquid in Dutch oven over medium-high heat about 20 minutes or until reduced by half; skim fat. Season with additional salt and pepper, if desired. Cut pork; serve with sauce.

Makes 8 servings

Spicy-Sweet Lamb Tagine with Saffron Couscous

- 1 tablespoon olive oil
- 2 pounds boneless lamb shoulder or leg, cut into 1½- to 2-inch cubes
- 3 medium onions, cut into eighths
- 3 cloves garlic, minced
- 2 teaspoons ground ginger
- 2 teaspoons ground cinnamon
- 1 teaspoon black pepper
- 2 cups water
- 1 can (about 14 ounces) diced tomatoes
- 1 small butternut squash, peeled and cut into 1-inch pieces
- 1 can (about 15 ounces) chickpeas, rinsed and drained
- 1 cup chopped pitted prunes
- ½ teaspoon salt
- 1 medium zucchini, halved and sliced crosswise into 1-inch pieces
- Saffron Couscous (recipe follows)
- ¼ cup chopped fresh cilantro or parsley

1. Heat oil in Dutch oven over high heat. Cook lamb in two batches until browned on all sides. Remove to plate.

2. Add onions, garlic, ginger, cinnamon and pepper; cook and stir 30 seconds or until spices are fragrant. Stir in water and tomatoes, scraping up browned bits from bottom of pan. Return lamb to Dutch oven; cover and bring to a boil. Reduce heat to medium-low; cover and simmer 1½ hours, adding additional water if necessary.

3. Add butternut squash, chickpeas, prunes and salt; cover and simmer 10 minutes. Add zucchini; cover and simmer 10 to 15 minutes or until zucchini and lamb are tender. Remove cover; simmer until broth is slightly thickened.

4. Meanwhile, prepare Saffron Couscous. Serve stew over couscous; sprinkle with cilantro.

Makes 6 servings

Saffron Couscous: Combine 2¼ cups water, 1 tablespoon butter, ¼ teaspoon salt and ¼ teaspoon crushed saffron threads in medium saucepan; bring to a boil over high heat. Stir in couscous. Remove from heat; cover and let stand 5 minutes or until liquid is absorbed. Fluff with fork.

Forty-Clove Chicken Filice

¼ cup olive oil

1 whole chicken (about 3 pounds), cut into serving pieces

40 cloves garlic (about 2 heads), peeled

4 stalks celery, thickly sliced

½ cup dry white wine

¼ cup dry vermouth

Grated peel and juice of 1 lemon

2 tablespoons finely chopped fresh parsley

2 teaspoons dried basil

1 teaspoon dried oregano

Pinch red pepper flakes

Salt and black pepper

1. Preheat oven to 375°F.

2. Heat oil in Dutch oven over medium-high heat. Add chicken; cook until browned on all sides. (Cook in batches if necessary.)

3. Combine garlic, celery, wine, vermouth, lemon juice, parsley, basil, oregano and red pepper flakes in medium bowl; mix well. Pour over chicken. Sprinkle with lemon peel; season with salt and black pepper.

4. Cover and bake 40 minutes. Remove cover; bake 15 minutes or until chicken is cooked through (165°F).

Makes 4 to 6 servings

Hungarian Beef Goulash

¼ cup all-purpose flour

1 tablespoon Hungarian sweet paprika

1½ teaspoons salt

½ teaspoon Hungarian hot paprika

½ teaspoon black pepper

2 pounds beef stew meat (1-inch pieces)

4 tablespoons vegetable oil, divided

1 large onion, chopped

4 cloves garlic, minced

2 cans (about 14 ounces each) beef broth

1 can (about 14 ounces) stewed tomatoes, undrained

1 cup water

1 tablespoon dried marjoram

1 large green bell pepper, chopped

3 cups uncooked thin egg noodles

Sour cream

1. Combine flour, sweet paprika, salt, hot paprika and black pepper in large resealable food storage bag. Add half of beef. Seal bag; shake to coat. Repeat with remaining beef.

2. Heat 1½ tablespoons oil in Dutch oven over medium heat. Add half of beef; cook until browned on all sides. Remove to large bowl. Repeat with 1½ tablespoons oil and remaining beef; remove to bowl.

3. Heat remaining 1 tablespoon oil in Dutch oven. Add onion and garlic; cook and stir 8 minutes or until tender. Return beef and any accumulated juices to Dutch oven. Add broth, tomatoes with juice, water and marjoram; bring to a boil over medium-high heat. Reduce heat to low; cover and simmer 1½ hours or until beef is tender, stirring once.

4. Stir in bell pepper and noodles; cover and simmer about 8 minutes or until noodles are tender, stirring once. Serve with sour cream.

Makes 8 servings

Winter Squash Risotto

2 tablespoons olive oil

1 small butternut squash or medium delicata squash, peeled and cut into 1-inch pieces (about 2 cups)

1 large shallot or small onion, finely chopped

½ teaspoon paprika

¼ teaspoon dried thyme

¼ teaspoon salt

¼ teaspoon black pepper

1 cup uncooked arborio rice

¼ cup dry white wine (optional)

4 to 5 cups hot reduced-sodium vegetable broth

½ cup grated Parmesan or Romano cheese

1. Heat oil in Dutch oven over medium heat. Add squash; cook and stir 3 minutes. Add shallot; cook and stir 3 to 4 minutes or until squash is almost tender. Stir in paprika, thyme, salt and pepper. Add rice; stir to coat.

2. Add wine, if desired; cook and stir until wine is absorbed. Add broth, ½ cup at a time, stirring frequently until broth is absorbed before adding next ½ cup. Continue adding broth and stirring until rice is tender and mixture is creamy, about 20 to 25 minutes.

3. Sprinkle with cheese just before serving.

Makes 4 to 6 servings

Broccoli and Beef Pasta

1 pound ground beef

2 cloves garlic, minced

1 can (about 14 ounces) beef broth

1 medium onion, thinly sliced

1 cup uncooked rotini pasta

½ teaspoon dried basil

½ teaspoon dried oregano

½ teaspoon dried thyme

1 can (about 14 ounces) Italian-style diced tomatoes

2 cups broccoli florets *or* 1 package (10 ounces) frozen broccoli, thawed

¾ cup grated Parmesan cheese or shredded Cheddar cheese

1. Brown beef and garlic in Dutch oven over medium-high heat 6 to 8 minutes, stirring to break up meat. Drain fat. Remove to large bowl.

2. Add broth, onion, pasta, basil, oregano and thyme to Dutch oven; bring to a boil. Boil 10 minutes. Stir in tomatoes and broccoli; simmer, uncovered, over medium-high heat 6 to 8 minutes or until broccoli is crisp-tender and pasta is tender, stirring occasionally. Return beef to Dutch oven; simmer 3 to 4 minutes or until heated through.

3. Transfer to serving platter with slotted spoon. Sprinkle with cheese. Cover loosely with foil until cheese melts.

4. Meanwhile, bring liquid left in Dutch oven to a boil over high heat; boil until thick and reduced to 3 to 4 tablespoons. Spoon over pasta mixture.

Makes 4 servings

Old-Fashioned Chicken with Dumplings

3 tablespoons butter

3 to 3½ pounds bone-in chicken pieces

3 cans (about 14 ounces each) chicken broth

3½ cups water

1 teaspoon salt

¼ teaspoon white pepper

2 large carrots, cut into 1-inch slices

2 stalks celery, cut into 1-inch slices

8 to 10 pearl onions, peeled

¼ pound small mushrooms, cut into halves

Parsley Dumplings (recipe follows)

½ cup frozen peas, thawed and drained

1. Melt butter in 6- to 8-quart Dutch oven over medium-high heat. Add chicken; cook until browned on all sides.

2. Add broth, water, salt and pepper; bring to a boil over high heat. Reduce heat to low; cover and simmer 15 minutes. Add carrots, celery, onions and mushrooms; cover and simmer 40 minutes or until chicken and vegetables are tender.

3. Prepare Parsley Dumplings. When chicken is tender, skim fat from broth. Stir in peas. Drop dumpling mixture into broth, making 12 dumplings. Cover and simmer 15 to 20 minutes or until dumplings are firm to the touch and toothpick inserted into centers comes out clean.

Makes 6 servings

Parsley Dumplings: Sift 2 cups all-purpose flour, 4 teaspoons baking powder and 1 teaspoon salt into medium bowl. Cut in 5 tablespoons cold butter with pastry blender or two knives until mixture resembles coarse meal. Make well in center; pour in 1 cup milk. Add 2 tablespoons chopped fresh parsley; stir with fork until mixture forms a ball.

Pulled Pork Sandwiches

2 tablespoons coarse salt	1½ cups stout
2 tablespoons packed brown sugar	½ cup cider vinegar
2 tablespoons paprika	6 to 8 large hamburger buns, split
1 teaspoon dry mustard	¾ cup barbecue sauce
1 teaspoon black pepper	
1 boneless pork shoulder roast (about 3 pounds)	

1. Preheat oven to 325°F. Combine salt, brown sugar, paprika, mustard and pepper in small bowl; mix well. Rub into pork.

2. Place pork in Dutch oven. Pour stout and vinegar over pork.

3. Cover and bake 3 hours or until pork is fork-tender. Let stand 15 to 30 minutes or until cool enough to handle.

4. Remove pork to cutting board; shred with two forks. Serve on buns with barbecue sauce.

Makes 6 to 8 servings

Turkey Noodle Soup

3 pounds turkey thighs, wings and necks

8 cups water

5 carrots, coarsely chopped, divided

1 onion, quartered

1 teaspoon salt

¼ teaspoon dried thyme

¼ teaspoon dried sage

1 can (about 14 ounces) chicken broth

6 ounces uncooked egg noodles

Chopped fresh parsley

1. Place turkey in Dutch oven. Add water, 2 carrots, onion, salt, thyme and sage; bring to a boil over high heat. Reduce heat to medium-low; cover and simmer 1 hour.

2. Add broth to Dutch oven; simmer, uncovered, 30 minutes or until turkey is fork-tender. Remove turkey and vegetables from broth; discard vegetables. Remove meat from bones; discard skin and bones. Cut turkey into bite-size pieces.

3. Return broth to a boil over medium heat. Add turkey, remaining 3 carrots and noodles; simmer, uncovered, 10 minutes or until noodles are tender. Adjust seasoning, if desired. Stir in parsley.

Makes about 6 servings

Guinness Beef Stew

3 tablespoons vegetable oil, divided

3 pounds boneless beef chuck roast, cut into 1-inch pieces

2 medium onions, chopped

2 stalks celery, chopped

3 tablespoons all-purpose flour

1 tablespoon minced garlic

1 tablespoon tomato paste

2 teaspoons chopped fresh thyme

1½ teaspoons salt

½ teaspoon black pepper

1 bottle (about 11 ounces) Guinness

1 cup reduced-sodium beef broth

3 carrots, cut into 1-inch pieces

4 small turnips (12 ounces), peeled and cut into 1-inch pieces

4 medium Yukon Gold potatoes (1 pound), peeled and cut into 1-inch pieces

¼ cup finely chopped fresh parsley

1. Preheat oven to 350°F. Heat 2 tablespoons oil in Dutch oven over medium-high heat until almost smoking. Cook beef in two batches about 10 minutes or until browned on all sides. Remove to plate.

2. Add remaining 1 tablespoon oil to Dutch oven; heat over medium heat. Add onions and celery; cook about 10 minutes or until onions are translucent, stirring occasionally. Add flour, garlic, tomato paste, thyme, salt and pepper; cook and stir 1 minute. Stir in Guinness, scraping up browned bits from bottom of pan. Return beef to Dutch oven; stir in broth.

3. Cover and bake 1 hour. Stir in carrots, turnips and potatoes; cover and bake about 1 hour 20 minutes or until beef and vegetables are tender. Stir in parsley.

Makes 6 servings

Beer-Braised Osso Bucco

½ cup all-purpose flour

1 teaspoon salt

½ teaspoon black pepper

4 veal shanks (about 3 pounds), cut into 1-inch rounds

3 tablespoons canola oil

3 carrots, chopped

3 stalks celery, chopped

1 large onion, sliced

2 cloves garlic, minced

2 tablespoons tomato paste

1 bottle (12 ounces) beer

2 cups beef broth

1 whole bay leaf

Grated peel of 1 lemon

Additional salt and black pepper

Hot cooked mashed potatoes or cooked polenta (optional)

Chopped fresh parsley (optional)

1. Preheat oven to 325°F. Combine flour, 1 teaspoon salt and ½ teaspoon pepper in medium bowl. Add veal; turn to coat.

2. Heat oil in Dutch oven over medium-high heat. Cook veal shanks, two at a time, 4 to 6 minutes or until browned on both sides. Remove to plate. Add carrots, celery and onion to Dutch oven; cook and stir over medium heat about 5 minutes or until vegetables are softened. Add garlic; cook and stir 1 minute. Stir in tomato paste. Stir in beer, scraping up browned bits from bottom of pan. Return veal to Dutch oven.

3. Add broth, bay leaf and lemon peel to Dutch oven; season with additional salt and pepper. Bring to a boil over high heat.

4. Cover and bake 2½ to 3 hours or until veal is fork-tender. Remove veal to platter. Strain liquid in Dutch oven; boil until reduced to about 2 cups. Serve veal with sauce and potatoes, if desired. Garnish with parsley.

Makes 4 servings

Five Mushroom Risotto

4 cups vegetable broth

4 tablespoons olive oil, divided

2 tablespoons butter

1 shallot, minced

¼ cup fresh Italian parsley, minced

¼ cup dry white wine

½ cup *each* shiitake, chanterelle, portobello, oyster and button mushrooms, wiped clean and chopped into ½-inch pieces

½ teaspoon coarse salt

1 cup uncooked arborio rice

½ cup whipping cream

¼ cup grated Parmesan cheese

Salt and black pepper

White truffle oil (optional)

1. Bring broth to a boil in medium saucepan over medium-high heat. Reduce heat to low; keep warm.

2. Heat 2 tablespoons oil and butter in Dutch oven over medium-high heat. Add shallot; cook and stir 30 seconds or just until beginning to brown. Add parsley; cook and stir 30 seconds.

3. Add wine; cook and stir until wine evaporates. Add mushrooms and coarse salt; cook and stir until mushrooms have softened and reduced their volume by half. Spoon mushroom mixture into medium bowl; set aside.

4. Heat remaining 2 tablespoons oil in Dutch oven. Add rice; cook and stir 1 to 2 minutes or until edges of rice become translucent.

5. Reduce heat to medium-low. Add broth, ½ cup at a time, stirring frequently until broth is absorbed before adding next ½ cup. Continue adding broth and stirring until only ½ cup broth remains. Stir mushroom mixture into rice. Add remaining broth; cook and stir until absorbed.

6. Remove from heat. Add cream and cheese; stir until cheese is melted. Season with salt and pepper. Drizzle with truffle oil, if desired.

Makes 4 servings

Southern-Style Chicken and Greens

1 teaspoon salt

1 teaspoon paprika

½ teaspoon black pepper

3½ pounds bone-in chicken pieces

4 thick slices smoked bacon (4 ounces), cut into ¼-inch strips

1 cup uncooked rice

1 can (about 14 ounces) stewed tomatoes, undrained

1¼ cups chicken broth

2 cups packed coarsely chopped fresh collard or mustard greens or kale (3 to 4 ounces)

1. Preheat oven to 350°F. Combine salt, paprika and pepper in small bowl; sprinkle over chicken.

2. Cook and stir bacon in Dutch oven over medium heat until crisp. Drain on paper towel-lined plate. Add chicken in batches to drippings in Dutch oven; cook about 10 minutes or until browned on all sides. (Cook chicken in single layer; do not crowd pieces.) Remove to plate. Drain all but 1 tablespoon drippings.

3. Add rice to drippings; cook and stir 1 minute. Add tomatoes with juice, broth, collard greens and half of bacon; bring to a boil over high heat. Remove from heat; arrange chicken over rice mixture.

4. Cover and bake about 40 minutes or until chicken is cooked through (165°F) and most of liquid is absorbed. Let stand 5 minutes before serving. Sprinkle with remaining bacon.

Makes 4 to 6 servings

Espresso-Laced Pot Roast

2 tablespoons
all-purpose flour

1 tablespoon espresso
powder

1 tablespoon packed
brown sugar

½ teaspoon salt

½ teaspoon black pepper

1 (2- to 2½-pound) boneless
beef chuck pot roast

1½ tablespoons vegetable oil
or bacon drippings

1 can (about 14 ounces)
beef broth

1 large onion, coarsely
chopped

1 pound carrots, cut
into 1-inch pieces

6 to 8 red potatoes,
cut into quarters

Chopped fresh parsley
(optional)

1. Preheat oven to 350°F. Combine flour, espresso, brown sugar, salt and pepper in small bowl. Rub all sides of pot roast with flour mixture.

2. Heat oil in large Dutch oven over medium heat. Add beef; cook about 5 minutes or until bottom is browned. Turn and cook 3 to 4 minutes or until browned. Stir in broth and onion.

3. Cover and bake 1 hour. Turn beef; add carrots and potatoes. Cover and bake about 1 hour or until beef and vegetables are fork-tender. Remove beef to cutting board; tent with foil and let stand 5 minutes.

4. Cook liquid and vegetables in Dutch oven over high heat until reduced and slightly thickened. Slice beef; return to Dutch oven. Garnish with parsley.

Makes 6 to 8 servings

Acknowledgments

The publisher would like to thank the companies and organizations
listed below for the use of their recipes and photographs in this publication.

Campbell Soup Company

Cream of Wheat® Cereal, A Division of B&G Foods North America, Inc.

®Johnsonville Sausage, LLC

National Pork Board

Nestlé USA

Ortega®, A Division of B&G Foods
North America, Inc.

Recipes courtesy of the Reynolds Kitchens

Riviana Foods Inc.

Sargento® Foods Inc.

USA Rice Federation®

Index

Index

Index

Metric Conversion Chart

VOLUME MEASUREMENTS (dry)

$^1/_8$ teaspoon = 0.5 mL
$^1/_4$ teaspoon = 1 mL
$^1/_2$ teaspoon = 2 mL
$^3/_4$ teaspoon = 4 mL
1 teaspoon = 5 mL
1 tablespoon = 15 mL
2 tablespoons = 30 mL
$^1/_4$ cup = 60 mL
$^1/_3$ cup = 75 mL
$^1/_2$ cup = 125 mL
$^2/_3$ cup = 150 mL
$^3/_4$ cup = 175 mL
1 cup = 250 mL
2 cups = 1 pint = 500 mL
3 cups = 750 mL
4 cups = 1 quart = 1 L

VOLUME MEASUREMENTS (fluid)

1 fluid ounce (2 tablespoons) = 30 mL
4 fluid ounces ($^1/_2$ cup) = 125 mL
8 fluid ounces (1 cup) = 250 mL
12 fluid ounces (1$^1/_2$ cups) = 375 mL
16 fluid ounces (2 cups) = 500 mL

WEIGHTS (mass)

$^1/_2$ ounce = 15 g
1 ounce = 30 g
3 ounces = 90 g
4 ounces = 120 g
8 ounces = 225 g
10 ounces = 285 g
12 ounces = 360 g
16 ounces = 1 pound = 450 g

DIMENSIONS

$^1/_{16}$ inch = 2 mm
$^1/_8$ inch = 3 mm
$^1/_4$ inch = 6 mm
$^1/_2$ inch = 1.5 cm
$^3/_4$ inch = 2 cm
1 inch = 2.5 cm

OVEN TEMPERATURES

250°F = 120°C
275°F = 140°C
300°F = 150°C
325°F = 160°C
350°F = 180°C
375°F = 190°C
400°F = 200°C
425°F = 220°C
450°F = 230°C

BAKING PAN SIZES

Utensil	Size in Inches/Quarts	Metric Volume	Size in Centimeters
Baking or Cake Pan (square or rectangular)	8×8×2	2 L	20×20×5
	9×9×2	2.5 L	23×23×5
	12×8×2	3 L	30×20×5
	13×9×2	3.5 L	33×23×5
Loaf Pan	8×4×3	1.5 L	20×10×7
	9×5×3	2 L	23×13×7
Round Layer Cake Pan	8×1½	1.2 L	20×4
	9×1½	1.5 L	23×4
Pie Plate	8×1¼	750 mL	20×3
	9×1¼	1 L	23×3
Baking Dish or Casserole	1 quart	1 L	—
	1½ quart	1.5 L	—
	2 quart	2 L	—